Barcode in Back

MANAGING CUSTOMERS THROUGH ECONOMIC CYCLES

MANAGING CUSTOMERS THROUGH ECONOMIC CYCLES

John McKean

WILEY

A John Wiley & Sons, Ltd., Publication

Registered office
John Wiley & Sons Ltd, The Atrium, Southern Gate, Chichester, West Sussex,
PO19 8SQ, United Kingdom

For details of our global editorial offices, for customer services and for
information about how to apply for permission to reuse the copyright material
in this book please see our website at www.wiley.com.

Library of Congress Cataloging-in-Publication Data

McKean, John, 1956–
    Managing customers through economic cycles / John McKean.
       p. cm.
    Includes bibliographical references and index.
    ISBN 978-0-470-68620-1 (cloth)
    1. Customer relations. 2. Consumer behavior. 3. Business cycles.
4. Recessions. I. Title.
    HF5415.5.M3853 2010
    658.8'12–dc22   2009049241

A catalogue record for this book is available from the British Library.
ISBN 978-0-470-68620-1

Set in 12/15 pt Garamond by Toppan Best-set Premedia Limited
Printed in Great Britain by TJ International Ltd, Padstow, Cornwall, UK

Contents

Acknowledgements

I am honored by and appreciative of the following friends, colleagues, and advisors whose time and insight shaped the ideas contained in this book.

Thanks to Patti Wilson, Rick Schaefer, Val Swisher, Mike Lofton, Ben Marbury, Tom Pencek, Bob Karr, Mitchell Levy, Daniel Chow, Ilmar Taimre, George Zdanowicz, Paul Bowers, Paul Dickson, Wendy Eggleton, Ann Nolan, Ryan MacNeil, Debbi Bowes, Joni Newkirk, Barbara Higgins, Ed Baklor, Priscilla Trumbull, Chris Holling, Behravesh Nariman, John Quinn, Iain Henderson, Donna Knoop, Trevor Dukes, Erik Koik, and Dave Schardt.

Several people listed above helped shape my thinking, but corporate sensitivities required their organization names and specific references be withheld. Special thanks to Ilmar Taimre for his and his team's support in this book. Also a special acknowledgement of Ray Kordupleski's ground-breaking work. Special thanks to my long-time colleague and advisor, Wendy Eggleton, whose insight, clear thinking, and editing helped immeasurably in structuring this book's ideas and delivery.

1 Introduction

Business's greatest customer opportunities and risks are determined by how well customers are managed through economic cycles. Despite the fact that 65% of a business's existence is managing customers in hyper-competitive economic transitions, it is predominated by reactionary approaches and guesswork.

Whether it is how consumers change their buying behaviors or how businesses change their spending behavior through economic cycles and transitions, they both are predictable and addressable.

This book focuses on the unique business knowledge, skills, and underlying disciplines to enable any business to optimally address these distinct customer opportunities, challenges, and risks created as customers' transition through economic cycles.

For the past decade, many industrialized nations have experienced strong growth with an unprecedented availability of financial resources. This fueled excess expenditures bordering on decadence. It was a sharp contrast to the Great Depression, the biggest crisis experienced by the world economy. Boom and bust are extremes in the continuum of economic cycles and each generates specific consumer behaviors.

If we hearken back to previous generations especially "depression babies" spending was characteristically stoic with patience and endurance toward one's lifestyle, i.e. if they didn't have it, they didn't spend it.

This is in direct contrast to behaviors during these recent boom times. Consumers conspicuously consumed. They were able to leverage homes and other assets to gain access to extra money and so have been able to purchase more. However, they were also able to go further into debt. Credit cards have enabled us to spend more money than we actually earn. From a behavioral perspective, this has created an expectation of material entitlement beyond that which most generations could typically afford.

During 2008, the economy tanked. Real estate plummeted. People's life savings were shattered, i.e. cut in half. Jobless claims reached a 26-year high. Consumers' behaviors changed, and changed quickly.

What happened to businesses? What happened to their customers? Those businesses that were prepared and able to proactively use the economic turn as an opportunity flourished. Those that weren't struggled to survive and in some cases, disappeared.

What was the difference?

That was the question we asked ourselves. So following the 2008 melt-down, we at the Centre for Information Based Competition started tracking:

- Consumer behavioral changes
- Business behavioral changes
- Businesses' response to behavioral changes
- How business changed buying behavior.

And using that data determined which core business competencies were critical to sustained success during changing economic times.

Research methodology

The research was global in its nature. It crossed numerous industries including but not limited to: financial services, telco's, retailers, travel, manufacturing, and consumer goods. Both small businesses and Fortune 100 companies were tracked. To that mix we added insights from consumers, business leaders, and economic forecasters.

Key findings

The research showed that there are three areas where successful and disappearing businesses differ:

- The first is in understanding the science of their customers' buying behaviors. This includes knowing who their customers are and how they're feeling. It also includes how the drivers of a buying decision changes as economic factors change.
- Second is leveraging loyalty within their consumer base. This requires a thorough understanding of the different kinds of loyalty and the financial benefits of each.
- And third is maximizing the core business competencies to not only proactively adapt but to use the changes that occur within the economy.

Beyond these three key areas of difference, the research also illustrated how "community" is playing an ever-increasing role in the success of businesses. This includes the physical communities. It also includes the virtual community. It's the latter that is having significant impact on how customers and businesses interact, particularly during these changing economic times.

Summary

Economic cycles have both boom and bust periods. Businesses seeking long-term success need to thrive in all economic environments. Those companies who continue to achieve this have done so by having their core business competencies focused on meeting the predictable customer changes in a way that continues to leverage loyalty.

Simple – but how do they do it?

We have split the book into 10 chapters (Chapter 1 being the Introduction, and Chapter 10 a Summary) to answer that question.

Chapter 2 – Predicting/Preparing for Economic Transitions: How businesses can best predict and then prepare for any economic transition or cycle.

Chapter 3 – Science of How Consumers' Buying Changes over Cycles: How consumers' buying changes relative to (a) reprioritization of needs, (b) changes in how they perceive value, (c) in the context of how economic conditions influence (a) and (b).

Chapter 4 – Consumer Loyalty Strengths/Vulnerabilities in Cycles: How different loyalty types endure varying economic conditions.

Chapter 5 – B2C Approaches for Dynamic Consumer Needs/Value Tradeoff: Proven consumer tactics optimized for different economic cycles.

Chapter 6 – B2B Approaches for Different Economic Cycles: Proven approaches, transformation strategies, and business case methodologies for economic conditions.

Chapter 7 – Mastering Information across Economic Cycles: Strategies and tactics for leveraging information to optimize business through economic transitions.

Chapter 8 – Managing the Employee Factor through Cycles: Strategies on managing employees through economic transitions and cycles.

Chapter 9 – Leveraging the Power of the Community (Physical and Online): Strategies and tactics for leveraging the physical business community as well as online communities.

By sharing our research learnings, we hope to help businesses get and keep customers through periods of boom and of bust.

Predicting/Preparing for
2 Economic Transitions

Understanding the macroeconomics which drive business cycles is key to developing a relevant strategy to manage through economic cycles. This last economic contraction, while not totally unique, followed an understandable pattern over past economic history. In this last economic downturn, some equated the business dynamics to a "hangover after a binge", i.e. economic contraction after a global liquidity binge.

Many parts of the world had experienced a long global liquidity bubble that was fueled in large part not only by home prices in the US but also in places like the UK, Spain, and Ireland. As well, factors of equity markets in places like China drove a big run-up in commodity prices not limited to oil (which may have represented the last hurrah of the liquidity bubble). Investors were looking for the next best place to put their funds as the housing market came crashing down.

We also saw a rise in oil prices from 2002 to 2007 driven via strong economic fundamentals. The end of that run was largely due to speculative commodity trading. This significant factor was intensified by the strong growth in China. As China came off a blistering run of expansion, investors started moving into commodities as the global economic conditions began to unravel.

Simultaneously, the binge on liquidity driven by greed came unraveled when the US financial markets began to fall apart. The US banks have had so many toxic securitized loans themselves that in itself would have been bad. But they had also sold such loans overseas to UK and European banks – e.g. in Austria, Sweden, and Spain. These banks in turn made loans to private sector borrowers in emerging Europe. Homeowners in places like Hungary started buying euro denominated mortgages, which added to the huge exposure of European banks and their subsidiaries. All these available funds for both lenders and borrowers encouraged everyone to take on risks – risks that they perceived to be very low.

Once the bottom started falling out of the real estate markets, the bottom fell out of the lending frenzy. Within regional markets, areas such as emerging Europe were spinning their own web of liquidity bubbles, e.g. Hungarian households were borrowing in euros and Swiss francs in hopes that they would hedge against exchange rate differentials.

This all may appear to be a unique perfect storm of economics … but it is not. History is full of financial and market calamities, which coincide with each other. It is a fact of business life. Bad economic and business cycles happen. Good economic and business cycles happen. All businesses can count on both in varying degrees of severity.

Historical examples

1620–1637 Tulip Mania*

Tulip Mania (or Tulipomania) is an extraordinary event in the history of cut flowers. It refers to a period in the Netherlands, in the early 1600s, where speculation on tulip

*Source: Melbourne Market Authority.

bulbs reached fever pitch resulting in extremely high prices being paid for single bulbs and the inevitable crash. People won or lost massive amounts of money gambling on the color of the flower produced by tulip bulbs, which in those days was unpredictable.

News of the massive profits speculators were making quickly spread, and by 1634 even tradespeople were becoming involved. One current day view on why this happened is that it was not caused by irrational speculation or greed, but rather by a Dutch parliamentary decree (originally sponsored by Dutch investors made wary by the Thirty Years War in progress) that made the purchase of tulip bulb "futures contracts" a fairly risk-free proposition.

Either way, this flood of new money caused prices to escalate rapidly in 1635, with many people buying on credit. By 1636 sales were structured by unofficial "colleges" or stock exchanges that held auctions at local inns. Speculation had also started on futures – in other words on the accessibility and price of bulbs at a specified future time.

It is problematical to convert seventeenth century tulip prices to modern currencies, as many were sold for livestock and houses. As an estimate, the average annual income in 1620 was about 150 Dutch florins. If we assume that this is comparable to $50,000, then in 1620, at the start of the tulip mania, a single bulb changed hands for about $330,000. Fifteen years later, in 1635, 40 bulbs were sold for 100 times this sum i.e. $33 million, or $825,000 per bulb. The record sale was in 1636 when a single bulb of "Semper Augustus", a striped carmine and white variety, sold for between 5000 and 6000 florins (depending on the report you read), which equates to between $1.67 and $2 million. The actual price for this small bulb, thought not to be of flowering size, was 4600 florins plus a coach and two dapple-grey horses.

The bubble ruptured in February 1637 when the soaring prices could no longer be sustained and there was a huge sell-off. Prices plummeted and many people were financially destroyed. While official attempts were made to resolve the situation to the satisfaction of all parties, their efforts were in vain. In the end individuals were stuck with the bulbs they held at the end of the crash – no court would impose payment of a contract, since the debts were judged to be sustained through gambling, and therefore not enforceable by law.

This was not the only time in history when flowers became the object of frantic market speculation. Smaller booms followed with tulip bulbs in Istanbul in the early 1700s, and in the Netherlands with hyacinth bulbs in 1734, and gladioli in 1912.

1720 South Sea Bubble*

The South Sea Company was a British joint stock company that traded in South America during the eighteenth century. Founded in 1711, the company was granted a monopoly to do business in Spain's South American colonies as part of a treaty during the War of Spanish Succession. In return, the company assumed the national debt England had built up during the war. Speculation in the company's stock in 1720 led to a tremendous financial bubble known as the South Sea Bubble, which financially destroyed many. In spite of this it was restructured and continued to operate for more than a century following the Bubble.

In 1720, in return for a loan of £7 million to finance the war against France, the House of Lords passed the South Sea Bill, which permitted the South Sea Company a monopoly to do business with South America. The company underwrote the English national debt, which stood at £30

*Sources: Wikipedia; http://www.historic-uk.com.

million, on a commitment of 5% interest from the government. Shares instantaneously rose to 10 times their value, speculation was rampant and a host of new companies, some fraudulent or just unrealistic, were launched. For example, one company was created to buy the Irish Bogs, another to manufacture a firearm to shoot square cannon balls and the most absurd of all "For carrying-on an undertaking of great advantage but no-one to know what it is!!" Incredibly £2000 was invested in this one! The country went crazy – stocks increased in all these new companies and other "questionable" schemes, and huge amounts of money were made. Then the "bubble" in London burst. The stocks crashed and people throughout the country lost their fortunes. Porters and ladies' maids who had purchased their own expensive carriages became destitute almost overnight. The Clergy, Bishops and the gentry lost their life savings; the whole country suffered a shattering loss of money and property. Daily suicides were common. The naive mob, whose inherent greed had lain behind this mass hysteria for wealth, demanded revenge. The Postmaster General poisoned himself and his son, who was the Secretary of State, avoided blame by unexpectedly contracting smallpox and dying. The South Sea Company Directors were incarcerated and their acquired wealth forfeited. There were 462 members of the House of Commons and 112 Peers in the South Sea Company who participated in the crash. Frenzied bankers crowded Parliament and the Riot Act was read to return order. As a result of a Parliamentary inquiry, John Aislabie, Chancellor of the Exchequer, and several members of Parliament were barred in 1721.

As these two examples illustrate, going from boom to bust wasn't necessarily about a lack of regulation or securitization. It wasn't about some bizarre form of derivatives. It wasn't caused by credit default swaps (CDS – credit derivative contract between two counterparties). It is easy to blame twenty-first century capitalism or modern finance but when businesses look to the longer historical context of what happened, economic cycles are almost a guarantee for every generation or couple of generations. Whether the discussion falls to Japan's crisis, the horrific South Korean financial crisis, Sweden (GDP dropped over 11% over three years), or Finland's financial crisis, modern history is also littered with examples of financial boom and bust. We have a tendency to believe that these are exceptional economic times when economies go horribly south but in fact it is just the natural evolution of human beings and society. It was about human nature, greed, and "follow the herd" instincts.

Emotional anchors from economic cycles

As well as stimulating the greed and herd instinct behaviors, economic cycles create emotional anchors. Recognizing these emotional anchors (or legacies) of economic cycles is necessary in understanding how consumers as human beings will react to current and future economic cycles.

The economic downturn that is most indelibly marked on the older population of consumers is the Great Depression. This economic cycle has indelibly shaped their lives and how they purchase. Even though they have lived through many eras of prosperity, these consumers' lives and how they stand was forever changed. For the over-30 population, most have experienced multiple years of prosperity and recessionary economies. The degree to which consumers' buying patterns are changed by previous economies is dependent on the severity of the economic cycle as well as the spacing between the economic cycles.

As one can see from the sequence beginning in early 70s, the US recessions have been relatively short in duration, which has minimized the emotional anchors caused by the constricted economy. While the recessions below are designated as US recessions, most of them have worldwide economic effects because of how closely many countries are tied to the US economy and the US consumer.

- 1973–1975 – oil crisis, stock market crash:
  ○ Recession Duration: 2 years
  ○ Years of previous prosperity: 13 years
  ○ Causes: A quadrupling of oil prices by OPEC coupled with high government spending due to the Vietnam War led to stagflation in the United States.
- 1980–1982
  ○ Recession Duration: 2 years
  ○ Years of previous prosperity: 7 years
  ○ Causes: The Iranian Revolution sharply increased the price of oil around the world in 1979 resulting in the 1979 energy crisis. This was caused by the new regime in power in Iran, which exported oil at inconsistent intervals and at a lower volume, forcing prices to go up. Tight monetary policy in the United States to control inflation led to another recession. The changes were made largely because of inflation that was carried over from the previous decade due to the 1973 oil crisis and the 1979 energy crisis.
- 1990–1991
  ○ Recession Duration: 1 year
  ○ Years of previous prosperity: 10 years
  ○ Causes: Industrial production and manufacturing trade sales increased in early 1991.
- 2001
  ○ Recession Duration: 6 months
  ○ Years of previous prosperity: 11 years

- ○ Causes: The collapse of the dot-com bubble, the September 11th attacks, and accounting scandals contributed to a relatively mild contraction in the North American economy.
- 2007 (Dec)–current
  - ○ Recession Duration: ?
  - ○ Years of previous prosperity: 6 years
  - ○ Causes: The collapse of the housing market led to bank collapses in the US and Europe, causing the amount of available credit to be sharply curtailed, resulting in a massive liquidity crisis. In addition, oil prices were high, stock markets crashed worldwide, and a banking collapse took place in the United States.

Note: Technically, economists in the US define a recession as two quarters of negative GDP growth. Officially, the beginning and ending dates of US recessions are determined by the National Bureau of Economic Research (NBER). The NBER defines a recession as "... a significant decline in economic activity spread across the economy, lasting more than a few months, normally visible in real GDP, real income, employment, industrial production, and wholesale-retail sales." From the period starting 1945–2007, the NBER has designated 11 recessionary periods with an average duration of 10 months.

In general, most short-lived recessions have minimal behavioral impact legacies 6 to twelve months after economic recovery. It is during the economic transitions that buying patterns will be tied to the emotional anchors of the previous economy. These emotional buying anchors manifest themselves in two primary forms.

The first economic transition behavior is a "wait and see" approach in terms of whether this economy is truly transitioning, e.g. "I'm not going to buy that new car until I really see things turn around", "I'm not going to sign up for that big vacation until I feel comfortable spending that much money again."

The second economic transition behavior is more opportunistic in nature in terms of looking for economic advantages in a particular transition, e.g. "Prices are dropping, it's a buyer's market; I should be able to get some good deals" or "I'm going to wait to visit my family until the airlines deepen their discounts." Or as Warren Buffet says: Be afraid when everyone is greedy; be greedy when everyone is afraid.

One travel destination business had created a premium travel service for 16 destinations around the world covering 10 continents. These all-inclusive vacations were geared toward a more affluent segment of the population. Shortly after the inception of this travel service, the economy contracted. Despite the fact that their business began with great success and garnered top travel ratings, they noticed their customer behavior changing not only in productivity in bookings but also in the timing of the bookings. Because of the nature of these high-end vacations, a typical lead time for a family to book a trip would be six to 12 months prior to the departure date. As the economy contracted, they saw a migration from eight months to lead times approaching 90 days. Many of the customers were used to booking their second vacations annually and no longer felt comfortable booking them so far in advance. The anxiety caused by the economic contraction had prompted them to postpone booking their vacation until economic indicators mitigated that anxiety. A portion of their customers turned into "hunters" which meant that they were now "hunting" for better deals on a holiday that previously they would have booked regardless of price.

Understanding the customer buying dimensions that drive such behavioral changes is imperative for a business to maintain relevance and business results during changing economic cycles.*

Economic forecasting

All businesses need to engage in economic forecasting to help predict what and how customers will buy. The key is not to view economic forecasting as a panacea but one of the tools used by businesses in visioning their future direction – the past is not always a predictor of the future. Not only will economic forecasts help predict behaviors relative to how much consumers have to spend, economic forecasting will also give the business an advantage when negotiating with suppliers.

Macroeconomic forecasts are also critical because of how interlinked not only industries but geographic economies are. Economic forecasting also helps manage not only a business's fixed costs but also what variable costs may look like in different economic cycles.

One of the biggest components is the labor force. The degree to which this can be managed in each business is directly related to the nature of the work force, e.g. unionization, regional employment factors, nature of work. Long-term forecasts are also critical to understanding what consumers will be evolving toward, such as what technology will be available or what type of cars will be driven in the future.

These strategic scenarios can span 20 to 25 years and be geared toward making strategic acquisitions whereas other short-term forecasts may be explicitly targeted toward spending over the next three months. These activities must be balanced with proactive scenario planning for a wide range of economic conditions. The reason for the balance is that

*Source: Wikipedia.org.

no one can perfectly predict the timing and severity of economic cycles but every business can create proactive scenario plans for economic cycles provided the scenarios have sufficient diversity.

In the last downturn, many businesses were lulled into a false sense of security that volatility had somehow engineered itself out of the classic business cycle. Much of this thinking came from businesses experiencing more gentle economic cycles lacking the volatility that existed in previous cycles. As a result, many of the scenario plans only addressed minor corrections in the economy. For example, many scenario plans' worst case scenarios contained a 15% reduction in revenues over six to 12 months. Many businesses in the last contraction experienced a 40% drop in revenues within 30 days. The speed and severity of this economic contraction was unprecedented. Scenario planning requests are now coming in not only for baseline, upside, downside but also disaster scenarios. This set up two powerful psychological predispositions.

The first was that businesses are now extremely fearful that future economic contractions will be as quick and as severe.

The second was that there is a growing fear that the speed and severity of economic contractions are largely unpredictable which creates an anxiety, permeating every facet of business.

Businesses were even debating whether the classic business cycle was dead. This makes future investment a higher risk proposition for businesses.

Plan for the likely business cycle while preparing for economic extremes

Most businesses plan for a range of economic scenarios with a variation of 15% either way. This variation is also planned to occur over a period of months, and not days. This thinking resulted from the economic pattern of recent history where business cycles trended shallower and shallower. The 2008 melt-down showed how both those parameters were insufficient: 15% was too little and months was too long.

Ben Bernanke, while Chairman of the Board of Governors of the United States Federal Reserve, referred to these phenomena as the "Great Moderation". Bernanke's "Great Moderation" or "the substantial decline in macroeconomic volatility over the past twenty years" was beginning to permeate not only the business managers' psyche but economic forecasters' as well. If this is, and forecasters believed that this was, "the way things were going to be" businesses could plan for just minor variations in their markets without risk of both extreme economic and business cycles.

This "Great Moderation" turned out to be only the "Great calm before the storm". Businesses grew increasingly complacent as business cycles moderated and inflation subsided. The only downside was that asset prices were beginning to get out of control e.g. home prices, real estate, and general.

Another economic tradeoff is the long-term effect of lower inflation and lower volatility in growth. Low interest rates for long periods of time create asset levels. These interest rates have been falling for a period of over 30 years. Consumers kept spending because credit was easy, and they counted on the asset prices, e.g. home prices, continuing to increase.

One of the factors in the extreme business cycle was not the event itself but the reaction to the events. Many consider allowing Lehman Brothers and AIG's downfall as a significant driver toward what caused that economic contraction to be so deep. As the economy contracted, the ripple effect of the financial system freezing up took what could have been a mild recession into a deep freeze. When one looks at the drop in the stock market from the 2001 recession, it was the worst drop since the Great Depression – yet the business cycle was mild.

Leveraging consumer lessons from previous economic cycles

On September 11, 2001, the terrorist acts in the US dealt a crushing blow on the US economy and globally. A major Canadian bank experienced a surge of investors pulling their investments out of the stock market after those investments had plummeted from the reaction to terrorism. This action crystallized their losses. The market then returned in three months to its pre-9/11 levels, having a devastating effect on those bank customers who withdrew from the market. In the downturn of 2009, the same bank didn't experience the same surge of investors pulling their investments out of the market because of what they had learned in 2001. At the same time, the experienced customer put less investment in the stock market and more in safe, guaranteed financial vehicles, taking the view, for example, that "I'd rather get 3% return than a negative return". There is an opportunity to use learning from previous economic cycles to create a marketing package showing the historic rebounds to educate consumers beyond their current fears.

Use consumer confidence data in context

Consumer Confidence Indexes (CCI) are indicators designed to measure consumer confidence in different regions and markets. Its goal is to reflect the degree of optimism consumers are feeling about the state of the economy with their savings and spending rates. There is not a global consumer confidence measurement because there is a wide variance of consumer confidence by country. There is an aggregated international consumer confidence measure that provides a glimpse of economic trends.

In the United States, consumer confidence is rated monthly by The Conference Board, which studies 5,000 households. The Consumer Confidence Index began in 1967 and is benchmarked to 1985 at a level of 100. This year was chosen because it represented a midpoint of economies. It is best to use this measure as one consumer barometer in the context of other market and industry consumer indicators. Many businesses argue that this is more of an art than a science as it is done with surveys and extrapolations of only 5000 consumers. Opinions on current conditions comprise 40% of the CCI with consumers talking about their future expectations being a full 60% of the index.

As a result, many nuances of markets are simplified and approximated. Also, the consumer confidence level is a more relative measure than it is absolute. Therefore businesses should not assume that the economic dynamics which create a certain numeric consumer confidence level are the same as in previous cycles. Other consumer indexes are tracked by the University of Michigan's Institute for Social Research.

Plan market scenarios based on a country's import versus export emphasis

Consumers have an inherent cultural bias toward the balance of saving first then spending. Governments also influence this with their emphasis toward the balance of imports versus exports. Governments will purposefully create export policies that promote domestic led growth rather than export led growth that will significantly impact consumer spending. This is to help isolate them from volatile changes in export dynamics. Asian countries as well as countries like Germany realized that any focus on export led growth created a huge risk and dependency on export activity. When exports dried up, these regions realized that an addiction to exports was as problematic as a new addiction to debt. It's imperative that a business understand its own import/export balance and how changing economic cycles will affect it.

Scenario planning

Businesses can make up for a degree of unpredictability in the economic cycles with good scenario planning. Every size of business should do scenario planning. Then they will have at least thought through the full range of scenarios. In this way, they'll be much better equipped to act and react – to doing what's needed to sustain through the tough economic times and to capitalize on the good economic times.

For the smaller businesses, they do not have the resources to spend on sophisticated economic analysis and forecasting. Therefore, it is best to go through simple scenario planning including extreme upsides and downsides.

For larger businesses, seeking outside expertize is a good investment to understand not only regional market issues but also global economic issues. There are also boutique economic forecasters that focus on particular niches within industries and regions. These forecasters are very helpful to define particular economic characteristics within niches.

Apply these 13 basic steps for scenario planning[*]

1. *Identify important questions of the business scenario*
   Assess whether scenario planning is the best approach to address the most important business questions. If the question is based on minor variations or a trivial number of elements, use more prescribed methods.

2. *Establish the time and scope of the business scenario*
   Consider how quickly changes occured over a period of time and assess the predictability of frequent trends, e.g. demographic shifts, product life cycles. Use time-frame ranging from one to 10 years.

3. *Name most important stakeholders*
   Identify who will be most affected as well as having an interest in the potential outcomes. Check whether and why these interests have changed over time.

4. *Chart fundamental business trends and driving economic forces*
   Include industry, demographic, economic, political, technological, legal, and societal trends. Determine to what degree these trends will affect your research question. Explain each trend on the basis of how and why it will impact the organization. Apply brainstorming in this process step. This allows all possible trends to be presented before they are assessed for feasibility, which enables solid group thinking and avoids scenario myopia.

5. *Identify key uncertainties*
   Chart driving forces on two x and y axes. Assess each force on an uncertain/(relatively) predictable and important/unimportant scale. Driving forces that are determined to be unimportant should be discarded. Key driving forces that are fairly predictable (e.g. demo-

[*]Source: Wikipedia.

graphics) should be included in all scenarios. This will create a list of important and unpredictable critical forces. Also assess whether any linkages between key forces exist, and discard "impossible" scenarios (e.g. full employment and zero inflation).

6. *Group potentially connected forces*
   Reduce key forces to the "*two*" most important to allow for a simple and understandable x/y diagram presentation.

7. *Map the extreme boundaries*
   Chart extreme boundaries beyond what the business thinks is probable for possible outcomes of the (two) driving forces. Assess these dimensions for consistency and plausibility. Three key points should be assessed:
   1. Time frame: compatible within the time frame?
   2. Internal consistency: do driving forces describe uncertainties that can build probable scenarios?
   3. Stakeholders: are any stakeholders in an unstable or imbalanced state relative to their favored state, and will this change the scenario? Is it possible to create viable scenarios relative to stakeholders? This is most important when creating macro scenarios where government policy or large organization politics will attempt to influence the outcome.

8. *Define the scenarios*
   - Chart two to four scenarios on a grid. The current situation does not need to be in the middle of the grid (e.g. low inflation). Certain scenarios may restrict one or more of the driving forces particularly when there are three or more driving forces. One approach's purpose should be to create all positive elements in one scenario and all negative elements (relative to current situation) in another scenario. After that, they should be refined while avoiding pure best-case and worst-case scenarios.

9. *Record the scenarios*
   Describe what occurred and the reasons supporting the proposed situation. Include sound reasons *why* changes have occurred. This supports the final analysis. Assign each scenario an unforgettable and captivating name for easy reference.

10. *Appraise the scenarios*
    Are the scenarios germane to the objective? Are they internally consistent? Are they the best example, i.e. archetypical? Do they represent reasonably lasting outcome situations?

11. *Identify market and economic research requirements*
    Determine where supplementary information is needed for each scenario. Obtain information relative to stakeholders' motivations. Identify promising future innovations in the industry.

12. *Make a decision on quantitative approaches*
    Develop models to quantify the scenarios that are relative to key metrics, e.g. growth rate, cash flow. This step requires a more specialized skill set than most of the previous steps.

13. *Integrate decision scenarios*
    Review each of the prior steps in an iterative process until scenarios are reached which address the essential issues challenging the organization. Assess both the upside and downside of each scenario.

Systematically monitor future oriented business cycle indicators

In most major downturns, most businesses significantly underestimated the severity of the economic conditions and the impact on their businesses. While scenario planning is a key aspect of preparing for tough economic times, it is only one tool available for businesses to leverage. An important group of economic barometers are financial indicators because the finance and credit environment creates the life-blood of any business cycle.

Key indicators are financial dimensions such as the risk spread between government bonds and the market. For the US, this would be US Treasury bonds and the market, e.g. junk bonds, commercial paper. This indicates how "tight" money and credit will be for businesses to invest. Another important group of business cycle indicators are the indicators that look toward the future. These forward oriented indicators are available in almost every country around the globe. The key is that these types of indicators capture what businesses are currently experiencing and believe they will experience in the future. It is the collective consciousness of where businesses "believe" their own business's markets, industries, and microeconomic environments are headed.

Institute of Supply Management Survey

An excellent example of one of these forward looking indicators is the Institute of Supply Management Survey published by the Institute for Supply Management (ISM).

The Institute for Supply Management (ISM) is the largest supply management association in the world and was originally founded in 1915. Their mission is to drive higher standards for the supply management profession through research, promotional activities, and education. ISM currently has over 40,000 supply management professionals with a network of domestic and international affiliated associations.

The Institute of Supply Management's Survey looks at many key indicators of economic and business cycle trending. The major categories of their index metrics are as follows:

1. PMI (Purchasing Managers' Index)
2. New Orders
3. Production
4. Employment
5. Supplier Deliveries
6. Inventories
7. Customers' Inventories
8. Prices
9. Backlog of Orders
10. Exports
11. Imports

These metrics are tracked by current month and previous month. They are also tracked by a percentage point change. In addition, there is an indication signifying the direction of the metric – e.g. contracting, expanding, increasing, decreasing – and a metric as to the rate of change as well as the number of months that it has been moving in its current direction (see Table 2.1). The survey also tracks overall economy metrics and the manufacturing sector itself with similar indexes.

The survey also offers narratives such as:

PERFORMANCE BY INDUSTRY

None of the 18 manufacturing industries reported growth in March. The industries reporting contraction in March – listed in order – are: Fabricated Metal Products; Textile Mills; Machinery; Chemical Products; Primary Metals; Printing & Related Support Activities; Transportation Equipment; Plastics & Rubber Products; Petroleum & Coal Products; Wood Products; Electrical Equipment, Appliances & Components; Food, Beverage & Tobacco Products; Furniture & Related Products; Nonmetallic Mineral Products; Paper Products; Miscellaneous Manufacturing; Computer & Electronic Products; and Apparel, Leather & Allied Products.

Table 2.1 MANUFACTURING AT A GLANCE MARCH 2009

Index	Series Index March	Series Index February	Percentage Point Change	Direction	Rate of Change	Trend (Months)
PMI	36.3	35.8	+0.5	Contracting	Slower	14
New Orders	41.2	33.1	+8.1	Contracting	Slower	16
Production	36.4	36.3	+0.1	Contracting	Slower	7
Employment	28.1	26.1	+2.0	Contracting	Slower	8
Supplier Deliveries	43.6	46.7	−3.1	Faster	Faster	6
Inventories	32.2	37.0	−4.8	Contracting	Faster	35
Customers' Inventories	54.0	51.0	+3.0	Too High	Faster	8
Prices	31.0	29.0	+2.0	Decreasing	Slower	6
Backlog of Orders	35.5	31.0	+4.5	Contracting	Slower	11
Exports	39.0	37.5	+1.5	Contracting	Slower	6
Imports	33.0	32.0	+1.0	Contracting	Slower	14
OVERALL ECONOMY				Contracting	Slower	6
Manufacturing Sector				Contracting	Slower	14

Source: The Institute for Supply Management (ISM).

In order to give their members the "gut feel" behind the numbers, they offer "telling" quotes which capture the essence of the metrics.

WHAT RESPONDENTS ARE SAYING ...

- "We remain challenged to align our capacities with demand." (Nonmetallic Mineral Products)
- "Most of the international markets have been reducing inventory levels and they are forecasting improvements in the next 4 to 6 months." (Chemical Products)
- "Many pockets of improvement." (Electrical Equipment, Appliances & Components)
- "Still very slow. No stimulus package for manufacturing. Down 30 percent." (Fabricated Metal Products)
- "What we are feeling now is that customers aren't making their final payments on equipment that has already been shipped." (Machinery)*

National Federation of Independent Business**

Another powerful future looking indicator is the survey published by the National Federation of Independent Business (NFIB). The National Federation of Independent Business is the nation's leading small business association. NFIB's network of grassroots activists send their views directly to state and federal lawmakers through a member-only ballot. This survey is probably even more forward looking than ISM's survey as it gathers the collective business "expecta-

*Source: Institute for Supply Chain Management, http://www.ism.ws/ ISMReport/MfgROB.cfm.
** http://www.nfib.com/page/home.

tions" and actual "plans" of what business performance and plans will be like in the near future. The small business members have a unique position in terms of having their "ear to the ground" and whose businesses are, in many ways, more dynamic than larger businesses. They refer to these index metrics as Small Business Optimism Index components.

Small Business Optimism Index components comprise:

1. Plans to increase employment
2. Plans to make capital outlays
3. Plans to increase inventories
4. Expect economy to improve
5. Expect real sales higher
6. Current inventory
7. Current job openings
8. Expected credit conditions
9. Now a good time to expand
10. Earnings trends.

They also calculate the total change of these metrics as well.

As Table 2.2 depicts, they record three dimensions of their index metrics.

This provides an excellent view as to where the business cycle is likely to go in the short term and enables businesses to gauge their markets more effectively.

Plan future economic cycles with risk probabilities

Every economic cycle has diverse risk probabilities. It is important to create a baseline of recovery scenarios with an upside and downside based on risk probabilities. During

Table 2.2 SMALL BUSINESS OPTIMISM INDEX COMPONENTS

Index Component	Seasonally Adjusted Level	Change From Last Month	Contribution Index Change
Plans to Increase Employment	–3%	3	–18%
Plans to Make Capital Outlays	18%	–1	6%
Plans to increase Inventories	–10%	0	0%
Expect Economy to Improve	–21%	–9	53%
Expect Real Sales Higher	–29%	–9	53%
Current Inventory	–5%	1	–6%
Current Job Openings	11%	0	0%
Expected Credit Conditions	–16%	–2	12%
Now a Good Time to Expand	3%	–3	18%
Earning Trends	–44%	3	–18%
Total Change		–17	100%

recessions, it is best for businesses to plan for three basic scenarios with the following symmetrical probabilities as a starting point:

1. Low/Moderate Recovery   60%
2. Fast Recovery   20%
3. Deeper Recession   20%

Factors that influence the direction and speed of recoveries range from influences of whatever factors led to the initial downturn, e.g. financial crisis, housing market, export interaction. These major factors plus additional external economy dynamics will impact the symmetry of the probabilities either up or down. This allows a business to plan for the appropriate level of either sales activity or cost containment relative to the direction and speed of the recovery. From these probabilities, other characteristics of the recovery can be estimated, e.g. regional differences, degree of reemployment, jobless expansion.

ID and monitor industry-independent "Canary in the Coal Mine" indicators

Some of the most helpful indicators for any business are those economic indicators that best predict a softening or strengthening of the economy prior to the actual business cycle directly impacting a business's market. These are referred to as economic close "canary in the coal mine" indicators. From early history, canaries were used as sentinels in coal mines to signal hazardous environments because they were more susceptible to a particular hazard compared to humans.

In business, certain industries or markets which are further up in the supply chain will be impacted at an earlier stage relative to changes in economic cycles. For example, the airline industry may be a "canary in the coal mine" to hotels or other vacation destinations. Therefore, hotels should be monitoring not only their industry but other suppliers to their industry.

Another dimension beyond where in the supply chain a business finds itself is also what position they are in the discretionary versus nondiscretionary spending of a consumer. Discretionary spending would be a leading indicator to nondiscretionary spending in a down turning environment.

In an improving economical cycle, the "canary" indicators would be reversed, e.g. nondiscretionary spending would stabilize and increase, then discretionary would follow.

While scenario planning can provide direction on what to do and when, businesses still need to be able to evaluate their actions and decisions with business cases. This is particularly true for Business 2 Business (B2B) companies.

At any given time, there are businesses booming and others going bust. In one B2B report, it stated typically (regardless of economic cycle):

- 30% to 40% of businesses were experiencing rapid to exponential growth.
- 40% of businesses were stable
- 20% were unstable or in decline.

Some business strategies work in one economic cycle and some are relevant to all cycles. Regardless, the first strategy for any business should be to understand its current economic environment while planning for the next.

Direct marketing to how economic cycles shift regional consumer spending

Economic cycles that are more severe than the average tend to reshape the consciousness of how consumers spend relative to pre-cycle levels. Following the very sharp downturn in consumer spending after the financial crisis in the US, US spending went from a global high to a global low. Conversely, US consumers' saving rate increased significantly as a result of the emotional and physical damage caused by the last economic contraction. In some areas of the world, e.g. China, Germany, and other parts of Asia, consumers in fact were saving "too much".

As economic contractions turn into economic recoveries, the best telltale sign is that the economic data starts to "bounce around" in the same place for a period of time while the economic "noise to signal" ratio stretches to flattening out. Once the recovery begins, it will be a shift in regional saving and spending rates.

This also depends on the timing of how the economic cycles traveled around the world region by region. For the US consumer relative to the consumer in other global regions, there will be a fundamental shift in saving and spending rates. The US consumer will likely continue to be a solid global consumer but not to the levels of consumption which occurred prior to the last liquidity crisis. This will come from any painful memory of US consumers tapping easy credit (credit is the lifeblood of the economy) and then getting burned in the process.

At the same time, as countries like China continue to recover and expand, China's consumers' saving rates will likely trend down relative to GDP while their spending expands.

These structural shifts in consumer spending will likely play out over a period of as much as 20 years. Long term, the Chinese consumers will, with all their spending, be a major force in the global economy as were the Americans for such a long time. This will be driven by the simple facts that there is a mass amount of Chinese consumers, that they have the resources to spend, and that they will likely spend those resources to improve their lifestyle. Conversely, the American consumers have recently been burned into stock market crashes coupled with a recent crash in home prices. The fiscal message for the US consumer translates into "We can't count on home prices going up forever, we can't bank on the stock market exclusively, so we need to more conservatively manage our entire portfolio with an emphasis on increasing our savings rate".

Strategic lessons learned

Our research revealed six critical 20/20 hindsights where reactionary decisions rather than sound strategic planning caused significant market and financial pain following a particular economic cycle.

"We cut marketing spend too far" Whatever you do, don't give up on marketing. When you cut marketing during a recession, you stop the conversation with your consumer. You are out of sight and ultimately out of mind, putting your brand at risk. The key is to rethink your strategy. Understand your current target mindset to make sure your message is relevant. Reallocate dollars to more effective mediums. Use this opportunity to build or strengthen your brand. A recession can be a great opportunity to gain market share and position your brand for the future. So don't just weather a recession – seize the opportunity to thrive. Continue customer development activities or pay the price in post-recovery economies.

The way in which a business or organization responds during an economic downturn sets their customer paths for future revenues. Many businesses experience the knee-jerk temptation to "batten down the hatches" during economic hard times. While this is a reality in many different cost dimensions of the business, doing this in a pundit Alan's fashion will result in significant revenue loss in the future. McGraw-Hill conducted a study which revealed that businesses that maintained their marketing efforts during the 1980–83 recession increased sales by 32% during the downturn and by 275% within two years of the economy's recovery. Conversely, businesses that cut back on their marketing lost 12% of sales during the economic downturn, and were only able to regain 19% in the same two-year post-recovery period.

"We sacrificed too much top-line investment for a bottom-line focus" Balance the focus between the top line and bottom line of the P&L. It is key during tough economic times to maintain a balanced perspective on not only the bottom line but the top line of the P&L. While it is critical to focus on the bottom line of costs during tough economic times, it is equally or maybe even more important to think about new and innovative ways to grow the top line. The talent: maintain the top line during economic contractions with an eye to how that will grow the top line in recoveries and onto prosperity.

"We shut down our organization's innovation by too much focus on cost-cutting" Keep top-line revenue innovation alive in tough times with an eye for better times. The natural inclination in tough times is to squelch top-line revenue innovation ideas with a bias toward a bottom-line focus. Businesses that follow this path will pay the top-line revenue price in good times. One wise, seasoned retailer sat down and interviewed with a prospective employee and asked him a strategic question: "What type of business person are you?

Are you the type of person who will put most of their energy into figuring out how to save four cents per hour on loading dock costs or how to use a cheaper wax on the retail floor? Or are you the type of person who is always after finding new innovative ways to grow the top line of the P&L?" This mirrors the conundrum that businesses find themselves in every economic cycle – what is the right balance? Each business's answer to this question is different, based on their place in the economic cycle.

One travel company continued to encourage innovation and new ideas for the top line while it shored up its bottom line. Their criterion for top-line revenue initiatives in tougher economic times was that the ideas would be economically viable for their customers in tighter economies but more importantly positioned them for strong revenue growth when the economy improved. One of the ideas they came up with was a travel product that combined "green" environmental activities with travel destinations. So instead of their travel customers just traveling to Africa on safari, they would schedule several days in advance of the trip helping villagers with local food and nutritional programs. This type of travel product fits nicely with the customer's psyche during tougher economic times.

- Require minimal amount of R&D
- Help customers feel better about spending vacation dollars
- Give travel business reason to communicate with customers
- Further investment could create strong top-line growth in recovering economy.

"We damaged customer experience by making bad choices in operational cuts" Protect your customer experience in

tough times. It is widely accepted that the customer experience is a significant driver for customer satisfaction and competitive differentiation. It is one of the key factors in attracting new customers, keeping existing customers, and developing cross-sell initiatives. Despite this, customer experience/satisfaction programs come under significant scrutiny when budgets are curtailed because of contracting economies. Businesses whose customer experience/satisfaction programs are the most vulnerable in contracted economies are those who have customer experience/satisfaction initiatives but not the deep and pervasive customer experience culture. One of the key reasons is that it is not an easy task to directly link customer experience/satisfaction metrics with short-term revenue generation and cost reduction initiatives. For the businesses that have an existing deep and pervasive customer experience culture, those initiatives continue to be funded as a priority even when economies contract. One large financial institution that had three major customer satisfaction/experience groups during a healthy economy ended up eliminating two of the three groups as a cost-cutting measure when the economy contracted. While this cost-cutting measure was successful at reducing costs, it did negatively affect customer satisfaction.

For most retail banking there are two key components.

1. Do it right
2. Do it quick.

In tough economic times, it is best to focus on the absolute most important customer satisfaction determinants and make sure that the cost-cutting initiatives do not impact these dimensions.

When the economy contracted for a major airline, their group in charge of advancing the customer experience transformed their efforts from promoting the customer experience to protecting the customer experience from other cost-cutting corporate initiatives. This group knew how critical the customer experience was in maintaining business levels in a contracted economy. As a result, they began funding efforts to educate other groups within the organization regarding the direct impact customer experience has on business levels. This initiative's focus was to measure the degree to which any potential cost-cutting initiatives would impact customer experience. Areas that were identified for potential cost savings were the mostly "creature comforts" on both business and leisure travelers flying domestic or internationally, e.g. free Hawaii Mai Tai for a leisure traveler on the flight to Hawaii, a hot meal in business class, a hot meal in economy class on an international flight, charging for a second bag for domestic flights. Of these suggested cost-cutting measures, all but the charge for the second bag were considered minimum requirements by the travelers when they flew this particular airline. The charge for the second bag was less a driver of customer satisfaction because most travelers could alter their behavior to avoid this charge. The impact was also mitigated by the fact that the entire industry quickly moved toward this as a new travel standard. The lesson is to identify the palpable and conspicuous core drivers of experience to the business and voraciously protect them from cost-cutting measures in tough economic times.

"We didn't plan our updates/refurnishing activities around economic cycles" Most businesses have operational components that need to be updated or refurbished on a regular basis. Optimally, these updates and refurbishing activities are best done when demand eases. While it is impossible to accurately predict the timing of economic cycles, there should be plans in place to sequence as much of the updating and refurbishing activities as possible during downtimes. One major airline took the opportunity during a recent contraction to refurbish their international aircraft because of

weakened demand. They also went further than this to expand the number of economy seats because of a shift in travel behavior, and added highly valued amenities to their premium cabins so that when the economy recovered, they would have a jump on the competition, with a truly differentiated premium cabin for a superior customer experience.

"We didn't recheck our consumer behavioral assumptions in the new economic cycle" Recheck your behavioral buying assumptions of your target market. Economic recoveries and contractions, particularly when they are significant, can cause fundamental shifts in buying behavior. In the case of a severe recession, relatively affluent consumers will adapt buying behaviors totally foreign to their previous buying behaviors. For example, affluent homemakers will begin clipping coupons where they have never done so before. Others will start subscribing to local magazines or news-papers just for the Sunday coupon sections. Refreshing your market research on when and how consumers are buying during transitions is critical to truly understanding what type of marketing and communication should be done if the business wants retention as well as creating effective acquisition strategies.

These consumer behavorial changes are never just one-dimensional. Many people have grown up with parents who experienced severe economic conditions such as the Great Depression. When these consumers are faced with similar severe economic conditions to those experienced by their parents, underlying sensitivities will be brought to the surface which will engage behavior that had previously lain dormant in their consciousness. For example, if a parent who experienced the depression era instilled a certain fiscal value system in their children, that grown child's value system will now have a higher consciousness triggered by economic conditions that harken back to the stories of their parents.

Science of How Consumers' Buying Changes over Cycles

3

The first step in understanding consumer behavior in any particular economic cycle is to understand the fundamental behavioral science of buying. In other words, what is the essence of how customers behave regardless of economy and then understand how that changes under specific economic conditions, e.g. hard times.

For example: During the recent downturn, the disappearance of disposable income drove a deeper concern related to employment or the lack thereof. This hits at the core of one's safety and security. Thus, a consumer's emotion can quickly turn to the primal need to survive. Suddenly, relatively affluent consumers are clipping coupons and going to auto wreckers. During a boom period, these behaviors would seldom happen. That primal need for survival, or at least the fear associated with it, virtually evaporates and other priorities take its place. But what priorities? And when? That is why it's essential for businesses to thoroughly understand the science behind customer buying decisions.

At the simplest level there are two core emotions that drive our propensity to consume. These are: greed and fear. However that is just the starting point.

There are Three Primary Dimensions (Sciences). These are:

1. How consumers satisfy their low and high-order needs.
2. How consumers rationalize their needs versus their perceived value tradeoff.
3. The economic cycle context and its relevant impact.

Low and high-order consumer needs

Very simply, consumers want the best product for them, at the best price, and during the sales and marketing (and service) process, they want to feel like they were known, important, respected, and trusted.

Rational Low-order Consumer + Intuitive, High-order Being

Consumers are always two-sided or hybrid "consumption" machines (Figure 3.1). They are:

1. Rational, low-order robot consumers
2. Intuitive, high-order human beings.

Figure 3.1

The rational consumption dimension of the consumer wants the best product for them at the best price (not necessarily the cheapest price). This is what drives researching product features and price shopping. This is also where the majority of businesses put the bulk of their sales and marketing activities.

The rational consumption dimension relates to rational choice theory. Basically, rational choice theory is that pattern of behavior in societies that reflects the choices made by individuals as they try to maximize their benefits and minimize their costs. In other words, people make decisions about how they should act by comparing the costs and benefits of different courses of action. As a result of these choices, patterns of behavior will develop within the society.

The idea of rational choice, where people compare the costs and benefits of certain actions, is easy to see in economic theory. Since people want to get the most useful products at the lowest price, they will judge the benefits of a certain object (for example, how useful is it or how attractive is it) compared to similar objects. Then they will compare prices (or costs). In general, people will choose the object that provides the greatest reward at the lowest cost.

The intuitive high-order human being side of the consumer wants to feel they are:

- acknowledged – known and important to the business;
- respected – for their time, diversity, needs, human dignity;
- trusted – by the business and trusting the business.

Most companies significantly underestimate the importance of high-order needs in the buying process. Consider that 57% of high-income customers who say they will walk away

What you sell vs. How you sell & service

Less than 10% of an institution's sales and service initiatives are focused on "people elements," yet that's why people buy.

Figure 3.2

because of bad service – that is directly related to their human high-order needs.

Together, the two dimensions (rational low-order and intuitive high-order) ebb and flow depending on economic conditions.

In troubled times, the consumer becomes more price-sensitive and therefore more willing to sacrifice the higher-order needs for the low-order rational needs. The shift is not radical but significant. In carefree times, the consumer splits the importance at about 30% price and product features, and about 70% high-order influences (Figure 3.2). When times are tough, the balance is about 50–50. The 50–50 split may appear understated as one would think that consumers would be radically price-sensitive in tough times. In many cases they are. But in relative terms, because most products and services are commoditized, the importance of price remains in check because the consumer has many choices of similar products at similar prices.

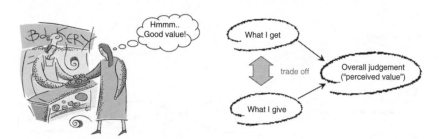

Figure 3.3

It's imperative for companies to understand the important mix of the rational consumption and of the intuitive higher-order needs (i.e. the weighting of each) and how this mix changes during economic cycles.

The value tradeoff

The second customer buying dimension concerns value – perceived value to be precise as value contains tangible and intangible elements. It is also very unique to the individual.

Fundamentally the value equation is: what I get versus what I give. The complexity of that equation comes with what each of those circles can contain. For example: the "what I get" obviously includes the features of the product or service. Not so obviously it can also include the expected lifespan of the product, the reputation for quality, and the status of the brand. Equally the "what I give" obviously includes the financial cost to buy. However it can also include the customer's time and effort. This makes the perceived value very individual as each customer puts a different level of worth on their time and their effort.

Perceived value (also known as the value tradeoff) is always relative as customers always have a choice (Figure 3.3).

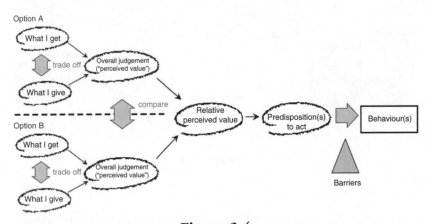

Figure 3.4
Source: Enhance Group.

That's why it's crucial that companies know their competitors as well as they know themselves (Figure 3.4).

Example: Family Dollar Store

An example of how this value tradeoff plays out is the Family Dollar company.

Some 14 million people enter one of Family Dollar's stores every week. Inside, they find something that resembles a hybrid of other retail outlets, with equal parts WalMart, drugstore, and supermarket. Customers can buy everything from groceries and cleaning products to clothes and motor oil.

Family Dollar spokesman Josh Braverman points out that the stores carry more name-brand goods than generics. "So we've put a lot of emphasis on kind of debunking the myth that if it's dollar store ... it's just going to break a day or two later. That's not the case," Braverman says.

Family Dollar serves both urban areas and small towns. Everything is not a dollar, but most products are sold in even dollar increments. The company's average customer used to make around $30,000 a year, but President Jim Kelly says that as the economy has worsened, wealthier customers have begun to stream in – "either out of necessity or perhaps they've paused to rethink some things as a result of the uncertainty of the economy". "That search for value is something that they're finding at Family Dollar and, as a result of that, more and more new customers are coming in," Kelly says.

While the S&P 500 declined by nearly 40% last year, Family Dollar's stock price jumped 36%. The North Carolina company even upped its dividends. The rare success, though, hasn't surprised Charles Bodkin, a retail and marketing professor at the University of North Carolina at Charlotte.

When consumers' incomes drop, "that drops the level of the type of store that you want to look at and shop at," he says. "Everyone's looking to save some money now. There's a lot of concern out there."

Bodkin refers to a trend called "trading down": when the economy goes south, consumers shop less at higher-end discount stores like Target. That's meant new customers for Family Dollar, and more spending from longtime shoppers like Telea Vinson, who stopped in for cleaning products.

"It's not where you shop, it's what you get," Vinson says. "It's the value of what you're paying for. And if it's the same thing you're paying for at Wal-Mart, I mean, you might as well come here and get it at a better deal." That's not to say Family Dollar always has the lowest price. The company aims to be competitive with bigger stores and then win over customers with convenience. Parking is almost always simple and checkout lines are short.

Bodkin says the recent success of so-called small-box stores shows up in earnings reports and word of mouth. "I had some friends who said they would not be seen in these stores because of the stigma that was attached to it," Bodkin says. "But you see quite a few people now, quite a few friends, shopping in the Dollar General, Dollar Tree, Family Dollar."

Family Dollar has tried to capitalize on the increased traffic by offering more of the things shoppers need and selling fewer of those they can live without. "It's kind of basic items that people say, you know, guest shampoo for the guest bathroom, guest soap for the guest bathroom, dishwashing detergent," says Daniel Butler of the National Retail Federation, "things that people use every day that they don't want to necessarily spend a lot of money on but they do want and need."

But what happens when the economy rebounds? Some – like Bodkin – say consumers will return to their old habits and Family Dollar's sales will fall. But Kelly, the chain's president, says that over its 50-year history, some of the company's biggest gains have come during times of economic recovery. And, he says, just because people will have more money doesn't mean they will stop looking for a good deal.*

Consumer behavior in economic cycle context

As with low/high-order needs (Figure 3.5), the perception of value is dynamic and changes within different economic cycles (Figure 3.6). Companies need to be responsive to these changes and, ideally, they should be ahead of the change. As Wayne Gretzky put it, skate to where the puck is going to be not where it is. In other words proactively

*Source: NPR.

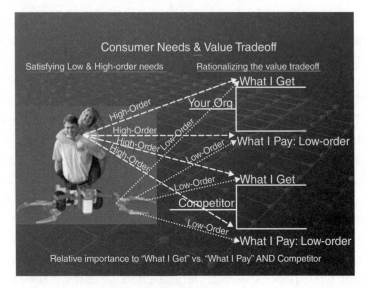

Figure 3.5

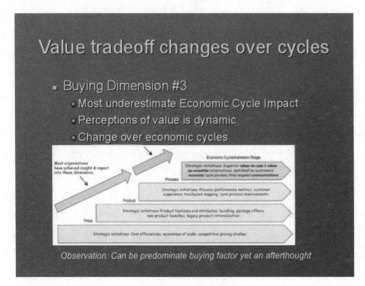

Figure 3.6
Source: Enhance Group/CIBC.

make the changes to meet the re-prioritization of your customers' low/high-order needs as well as their rebalancing of the value tradeoff.

For example: in contracted economies, consumers try to take on more of the service activities that they would normally purchase. This is a significant opportunity for most businesses to understand what part of their product and services are vulnerable to that "do-it-yourselfer" mentality. After assessing this, a bridge can be created to offer a halfway point for the consumer to help themselves as well as still retaining some type of revenue stream and relationship with the consumer.

For one law organization, they analyzed which aspect of certain legal processes a potential client could do for themselves with a little guidance from them. They steered the clients to certain self-help facilities to get them through the easier parts of the legal process. Once the client was at a point where it was no longer feasible for them to complete the easier aspects of the legal process, they would then engage the law organization that helped them through the self-help process. Satisfaction among the attorneys increased because many times the legal work that the client could do on their own was uninteresting and the type of work that was not particularly rewarding for a talented attorney. Standardized documentation for doing wills and estate planning are more popular during contracted economies, e.g. a franchise for litigation documents. Consumers are more comfortable with satisfying the minimum requirements of a legal document process when money is tight. They likely won't get the best possible outcome but it will likely be sufficient for their needs. For example, a full-fledged legal service would offer additional recommendations on tax implications and broader estate planning. The consumer will miss those additional "nice to haves" but they are not a requirement.

In the city of Halifax, Nova Scotia, Canada the contracted economy has significantly increased the number of people filing for divorce. As it is a time intensive and thus, potentially costly process, many folks started getting their "do it yourself" divorce packages which still were potentially confusing. Because of this, a local law organization office staff was completely consumed with fielding calls from people who were representing themselves in their divorce cases. To better manage this logjam and maintain the customer contact, they offered seminar style self-help legal sessions once every two weeks for people to bring in their own documentation and work through it under the guidance of the seminar leader.

By recognizing the changing mix of the customers' low and high-order needs, the law organization was able to simplify their work effort while maintaining their customers' business (albeit changed) (Figure 3.7). Or as one lawyer

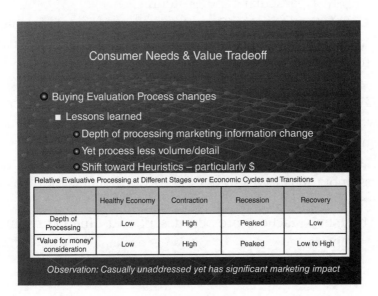

Figure 3.7
Source: Enhance Group/CIBC.

described it: "Sometimes you don't need to Cadillac, the VW will do just fine".

In trying to predict changes in customers' buying behavior, it's good to look at the various customer behavioral groups. Customers can be segregated into many different groups. One breakdown is:

- **Wandering Customers:** They have no specific need or desire in mind when they shop. Rather, they want a sense of experience and/or community.
- **Discount Customers:** They shop frequently, but make their decisions based on the price and the size of markdowns.
- **Impulse Customers:** They do not have buying a particular item at the top of their "To Do" list, but go into a store on a whim. They will purchase what seems good at the time.
- **Need-Based Customers:** They have a specific intention to buy a particular type of item.
- **Loyal Customers:** They generally represent no more than 20% of a business's customer base, but can make up more than 50% of their sales.*

Given that each group has a different motivation for its buying behavior it is understandable that when the economic cycle context changes so does the group's behaviors. In fact, the group differences can start to break apart and reassemble into two groups based on their reaction to the economic context.

These two reactions are best described as: Inert consumers and Hunters.

*Source: Mark Hunter.

Inert consumers

There is a large group of consumers in the market that would be defined as Inert consumers. The rough definition of inert is that it is a state of doing little or nothing. Most consumers buy with little effort or investigation. When the economic situation starts to change, the consumers who take a "wait and see" or "this will pass" approach fall into the Inert consumers group. Some Inert consumers however during times of economic hardship turn more dynamic in terms of their active thought process and effort in purchasing. They take on the "hunter" approach.

Hunters

There is a smaller group of consumers, relative to the Inert consumers, that actively and aggressively engage cognitive processing when buying. In the quest to predict customer behavior and determine loyalty, this group is the least loyal. This is a segment that is always seeking the best deal. Their belief is: "The best company gives you ... what you want, when you want, no matter what".

Their modus operandi is a series of evaluations, which entails absorbing a great deal of information. They are the ones willing to put forth the effort. In a downturn economy, this segment grows.

The various behavioral changes in consumer groups can be confusing and, if not well understood, put a business at increased risk during economic downturns. For example, to truly understand the underlying reasons why any business is experiencing a market share decline in sales, a determination must be made as to whether this is from a market contraction or a behavioral change. Beyond consumers following an Inert or Hunter-type approach to buying, a downturn in the economy can cause consumers to stop purchasing in certain categories. It can cause others to become "discount customers", changing their behavior towards bargain hunting, while others consumers will see the situation as an opportunity and will want to increase their purchasing. Such behaviors are driven by both fear and greed. Statistically, 30% of consumers are inertia buyers who will stay with a business regardless of the market conditions (sometimes because of switching barriers). That leaves 70% of customers exposed to the impact of the economic cycle.

Who are your customers and how are their behaviors changing? (Figure 3.8) Is it a market contraction or a behavioral change? Is the decline something you're doing or not doing or is it something your competitor is doing or not doing?

Successful companies who thrive in all market conditions can answer these questions with solid information and

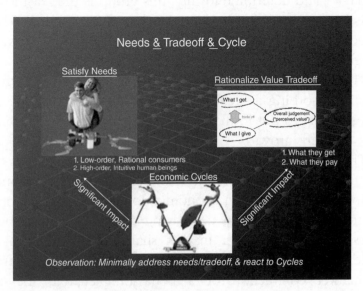

Figure 3.8

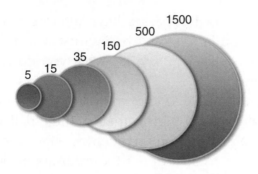

Figure 3.9

Source: Evolutionary Psychology by Robin Dunbar,
Louise Barrett, and John Lycett.

analysis. A key element within that information and analysis, and one that needs to be understood and monitored, is *trust*.

Trust is a component of the high-order needs and is especially sensitive to economic stress. When people are under stress, they spiral inward toward their smaller and higher circles of trust. Relative to Figure 3.9, consumers migrate from right to left when their economic welfare is threatened. Each progressive circle represents different levels of meaningfulness and trust in a consumer's circle of intimacy. In the most intimate circle of five, there are family members and very close friends. The next category of roughly 12 to 15 people would be regarded as the sympathetic group. Beyond the 150 circle, members would be known by role (e.g. politician or blogger) or by category as they relate to the networker (e.g. vendor or neighbor).

Trust is a long-term state of being, state of mind, and state of feeling. It is cultivated through ongoing behavioral engagement in incremental and conditional steps. The smallest group (5), by definition, had the most engagements where trust had been proven and therefore conditionally bestowed. Businesses can say anything in their marketing claims but until consumers or businesses have direct experiences at a human level, on an ongoing basis, trust will not be formulated. "It's not what you say; it's what you do ... and what you do over time."

To take an example: one of the core pieces of one manufacturer's value proposition is their on-time delivery of their products. Their current on-time delivery track record is 94%. Their strategy is to always tell the truth about delivery and "beat that truth". The CEO says there is nothing worse than committing to an eight-week delivery on a product and then delivering it in eight weeks and three days. Even though the three days might not make a great deal of difference, it is a missed delivery date.

When customers are under economic stress, the bar is raised on the trust continuum. Even though businesses many times assume that trust is implicit, it is not. It is something that must be engineered into products, services, processes, and everything that touches the experience. Under economic stress, the trust sensitivities are heightened. It takes more effort to increase trust, and fewer stimuli to decrease it. When businesses attempt to capture a consumer's trust, they are projecting out in the future how they will be treated or how the product or service experience will play out. When the actual product or service is experienced and the experience is different than that which was communicated, trust decreases. For example, many financial institutions advertise high levels of customer service, yet when the customer actually walks into the branch, the actual experience feels homogeneous and nebulous.

Without earning and keeping trust a business can't earn and keep loyalty. Without trust and loyalty a business will always struggle. Conversely, the greater an organization's capability to understand and manage trust and loyalty, the better its future prospects are – especially during periods of boom and bust.

In tough economic times, a market dichotomy occurs. Both consumers and businesses tighten spending yet both expect more "value" from their vendors and suppliers. This requires businesses to not only rethink their value proposition but to also reassess their competitors' value propositions.

The three key considerations of value propositions are:

• The value proposition itself
• The delivery of that value proposition
• The effectiveness of how it is communicated.

In all three of these components, consumers base their perception on the "two-sided coin" of value:

1. What they get
2. What they pay.

To understand the two dimensions of perceived value, we must look at both of these components and disaggregate them into the reprioritized elements relevant to the specific economic condition. These two valued dimensions must then be addressed in terms of the process of delivering and communicating the chosen value. In other words:

Step 1. Choose your new relative value – first, an organization must choose the new proposition value that is optimized for a downturn economy. In a downturn, both consumers and businesses shift spending toward safer and more proven products and services; i.e. the essential product and services.

Step 2. Deliver your new relative value – the second fundamental aspect of a generous value proposition is to ensure that you can actually deliver the value you chose to deliver. Both consumers and businesses are hypersensitive now to getting their "money's worth". If the value proposition is not delivered, their tolerance is almost nonexistent.

Step 3. Communicate your new relative value – the third fundamental aspect, and perhaps the most forgotten is communicating your new relative value proposition. Of the three fundamentals, this is the most underfunded and critical component.*

Consumers absorb a far more simplified version of your value proposition and the supporting marketing and advertising your business believes they have communicated. In communication theory, there is the old sender and receiver model. In the old days, the radio put out something and the consumers received it, i.e. you put out ABC, and the consumers received ABC. It was simple. In recent prosperous times, it's been complicated. So complicated that sometimes ABCDE is sent out and DCESB is received. Businesses need to realize they too can make their value propositions too complicated, too tricky, or too detailed.

When you start talking about brand imagery around certain products, such as Volvo is safe, Coke is fun, Apple is cool, IBM is trustworthy – it's simple. They have really simplified what their value proposition is.

If your value proposition requires that people really think about it and understand it, then it won't be very effective. It's not that they're dumb. They're not willing to put the time in because they don't have the time. You as a marketer have all the time in the world to think about your product and the nuances that are appealing. I'll give you a minute or two to think about your product and if it doesn't click in a minute or two, I'm not going to sit down and work through it. As opposed to something that clicks right away, they get somebody else's value proposition quickly.**

*Source: Enhance Management.
**Source: Wikipedia.

Communicating a value proposition

Businesses who try to communicate their value proposition by saying, "We appreciate and understand the tough economic times you're going through, and recognize your bottom line, and as a result of this, we are doing X" often miss the mark.

Value proposition scripting like this is pervasive in the financial industry with varying degrees of perceived sincerity. Somehow businesses think that consumers are naïve. That maybe they will believe this projection of empathy. They do not. In fact, it leads to a number of distinct cognitive and emotional reactions:

- You're lying to me
- You really don't care about me
- You really don't know me
- I'm unimportant to you
- You don't respect me
- I didn't really trust you before, but now I trust you a little bit less.

Therefore, it's best to be straight when trying to reach consumers. The following principles will help to achieve that:

- Deliver empathy realistically as to a stranger
- Be honest and straightforward
- Deliver your value proposition in simple quantified terms.

This is even more important during a downturn economy. During those times, consumers' processing gets simple (Figure 3.7). The use of heuristics and simple quantified messages works best. Heuristics allow you to provide a mental shortcut that lets consumers make a buying decision and judge options quickly and efficiently. Heuristics shorten decision-making time and allow consumers to function without much cognitive processing before buying (Figure 3.7). A majority of the consumers choose the easiest cognitive processing path.

Also during a downturn, customers increase their propensity toward fear-based buying. Therefore, the brand heuristics should be optimized for this type of buying.

In addition, in times of tight money, money is on people's minds. As a result, there is a general language shift toward monetary heuristics. These can either be in economic, financial, or accounting terms.

The desire code

In a broader sense, a business's brand heuristics creates a "desire code" consisting of simple, efficient rules consumers use which are hard-wired by evolutionary processes or are learned from experience. At a brand level, they explain how people make brand decisions, come to judgments about other alternative products, and solve problems. As the world is a complicated place, consumers use brand heuristics when faced with a complex situation or problem. They also use it when there is incomplete information such as when to buy a particular product or consider a service.

Heuristic rules work well in most circumstances but can lead to systematic cognitive biases. These cognitive biases are what brandings stand for. Therefore, it is important to resist the temptation to lower prices in a downturn economy because this telegraphs that the product or service is now of a lesser quality.

In the 1899 book *The Theory of the Leisure Class*, economic theorist Thorstein Veblen identified a propensity for people to perceive more expensive goods as being of higher quality than inexpensive ones (providing they are of similar initial quality or lack of quality and of similar style). Veblen also found that this holds true even when prices and brands are switched, i.e. putting a high price on an inexpensive brand is sufficient to create a perception that the brand is of higher quality than the normally more expensive brand.

Using Walker's desire code in the context of a downward economy, businesses must narrow the range of actual differences in commodity attributes. This is particularly important when money is scarce when attempting to create a value proposition optimized for tough times.*

Business to consumer value proposition fundamentals

Under a healthy economic, "carefree" consumption economy, the order of importance that the consumer assigns relative to high-order and low-order consumption dimensions is:

- 30% of the low-order dimensions are focused on "What I Get" and "What I Pay" (Figure 3.10).
- 70% are focused on the high-order aspects of "What I Get".

As in all buying decisions, the consumer always has a choice. Therefore, it's necessary to look at the relative choice schematic, i.e. "What I Get" and "What I Pay" as it compares with competitors (Figure 3.11). Again, there are high and low-order dimensions in both.

*Source: Stephen Byrne.

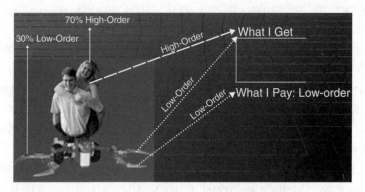

Figure 3.10

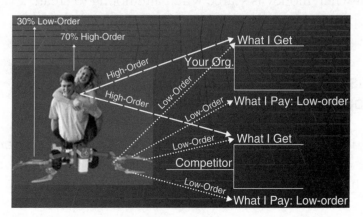

Figure 3.11

In order to redistribute the importance that the consumer assigns to the high and low-order attributes, we must disaggregate the "What I Get" into the business processes that deliver the customer needs, both higher-order and low-order. Then each is weighted as to its importance to the consumer.

Each assigned importance is relative to a main business process and to a product dimension. In Figure 3.12, the business processes that deliver the "What I Get" are typically

	Business Process	Customer Need	Importance
		Attribute 1	(40%)
	30% Product	Attribute 2	(20%)
		Attribute 3	(40%)
		Sales: Knowledge; Mkt: Relative to Comp.	(30%)
	25% Marketing	Sales: Responsive; Mkt: Simple	(25%)
	& Sales	Sales: Follow-up; Mkt: Relevant	(10%)
		Delivery Interval Meets Needs	(30%)
What I Get	25% Service	Does Not Break	(25%)
		Installed When Promised	(10%)
		No Repeat Trouble	(30%)
	15% Customer	Fixed Fast	(25%)
	Inquiries	Kept Informed	(10%)
		Accuracy, No Surprise	(45%)
	5% Billing	Resolve On First Call	(35%)
		Easy to Understand	(10%)
What I Pay			
		Competitor	

Figure 3.12

some form of sales and marketing, service, customer inquiries, and billing. Each one of those business processes delivers certain attributes of the customer needs.

For example, sales and marketing delivers a sense that the business knows the consumer, is responsive to the consumer, and is relevant in its product offerings. In service processes, this would translate to on-time delivery, the product arriving in good condition, and being installed when and as promised.

For the business process of supporting the customer inquiries, they ensured that there was no repeat trouble, that it was fixed and fast, and that they were kept informed of the repair. In terms of billing, they ensured that the bill was accurate with no surprises, that issues with the bill were resolved on the first call, and that it was easy to understand.

The next step is to measure the success of each of these internal metrics (Figure 3.13).

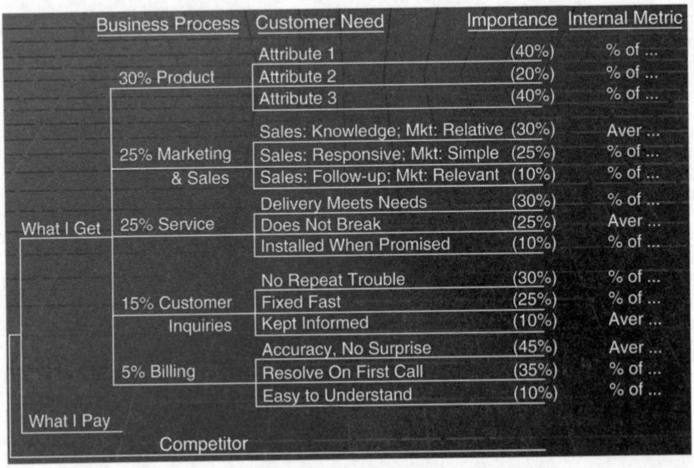

Business Process	Customer Need	Importance	Internal Metric
	Attribute 1	(40%)	% of ...
30% Product	Attribute 2	(20%)	% of ...
	Attribute 3	(40%)	% of ...
	Sales: Knowledge; Mkt: Relative	(30%)	Aver ...
25% Marketing	Sales: Responsive; Mkt: Simple	(25%)	% of ...
& Sales	Sales: Follow-up; Mkt: Relevant	(10%)	% of ...
	Delivery Meets Needs	(30%)	% of ...
25% Service	Does Not Break	(25%)	Aver ...
	Installed When Promised	(10%)	% of ...
	No Repeat Trouble	(30%)	% of ...
15% Customer	Fixed Fast	(25%)	% of ...
Inquiries	Kept Informed	(10%)	Aver ...
	Accuracy, No Surprise	(45%)	Aver ...
5% Billing	Resolve On First Call	(35%)	% of ...
	Easy to Understand	(10%)	% of ...

What I Get — What I Pay — Competitor

Figure 3.13

Value perception shifts in a downturn economy

In uncertain economic conditions where the consumer has shifted the importance of their needs from high-order to low-order needs, the relative importance shifts to product oriented needs.

This shift is significant but not radical when looking at product value. It also shifts within high-order needs as well. Once this is understood, the perceived value balanced between choosing a value and delivering the value can be adjusted and optimized for the sensitivities of a weak economy.

The consumer has a higher sensitivity level for product performance and service as well as billing issues. Not only does what the consumer deems important shift from the interactions to product (70% to 50% importance), it also shifts within interactions such as sales and marketing (25% to 10% importance), to service (25% to 15% importance), customer inquiries (15% to 15% importance), and billing/statements (5% to 10% importance) (Figure 3.14).

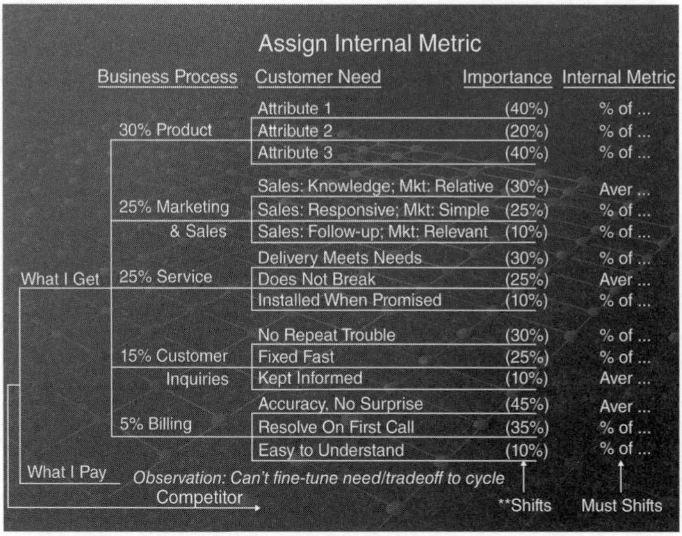

Assign Internal Metric

Business Process	Customer Need	Importance	Internal Metric
30% Product	Attribute 1	(40%)	% of ...
	Attribute 2	(20%)	% of ...
	Attribute 3	(40%)	% of ...
25% Marketing & Sales	Sales: Knowledge; Mkt: Relative	(30%)	Aver ...
	Sales: Responsive; Mkt: Simple	(25%)	% of ...
	Sales: Follow-up; Mkt: Relevant	(10%)	% of ...
25% Service	Delivery Meets Needs	(30%)	% of ...
	Does Not Break	(25%)	Aver ...
	Installed When Promised	(10%)	% of ...
15% Customer Inquiries	No Repeat Trouble	(30%)	% of ...
	Fixed Fast	(25%)	% of ...
	Kept Informed	(10%)	Aver ...
5% Billing	Accuracy, No Surprise	(45%)	Aver ...
	Resolve On First Call	(35%)	% of ...
	Easy to Understand	(10%)	% of ...

What I Get

What I Pay

Observation: Can't fine-tune need/tradeoff to cycle

Competitor

**Shifts   Must Shifts

Figure 3.14

Once these shifts in perceived importance of value are understood, then the process of choosing and then delivering the value can be engineered. The third component of communicating the value is the last critical link. It too needs to be reengineered for a downturn economy.

4

Consumer Loyalty Strengths/Vulnerabilities in Cycles

Getting and keeping loyalty is always a challenge. This is exponentially harder in changing economic cycles as loyalty also changes. It takes on different dynamics particularly when consumers are under economic pressure.

First, though, let's explore whether loyalty actually exists. The answer is yes. Loyalty does exist but what is it?

Is this "loyalty"?

- You're DuPont, and one of your customers is a chemical engineer buying polymers from you under a master purchasing agreement. He receives a volume-pricing discount. This customer represents a lot of revenue and repeat business for you, but is he loyal?
- Pfizer relies on physicians to prescribe its pharmaceuticals. One doctor admits that, all other things being equal, she specifies Pfizer drugs because she appreciates the educational seminars the company provides each spring in Florida. How loyal is she?
- A business traveler can buy coffee anywhere but seeks out Starbucks in whichever city she finds herself because she knows she can relax there. Can Starbucks assume it has created a loyal customer?
- An office manager gives Staples high customer satisfaction scores for breadth of merchandise, good pricing, and

friendly service. He also carries one of Staples' Business Rewards cards. Can we assume he's loyal?

- Nike has strong repurchase rates among amateur athletes who find Nike shoes a better fit for wide feet. Are these buyers loyal to the Nike brand?

Each of these scenarios describes a loyal customer. "Loyalty" comes in many forms. Should it be defined as a feeling? An attitude? A set of buying behaviors? It is all of this and more.

At the highest level, there are two umbrella loyalty categories:

- Behavioral loyalty
- Cognitive loyalty.

Behavioral loyalty is the simplest form of customer loyalty. This is where we see routine and inertia. It also typically reflects a weak competitive value due to the impact switching costs.

The following equations illustrate the situation:

$$\text{Value "supplier"} > \text{Value "competitor"} - \text{Switching Costs} \quad (1)$$
$$\text{Value "supplier"} < \text{Value "competitor"} - \text{Switching Costs} \quad (2)$$

In equation (1), the supplied value proposition is higher than the competing value proposition minus switching costs. An example would be an expensive food store close by. You may only prefer it because the less expensive food store is further away and thus would require more time and effort on your part. If the less expensive food store chain opened a new store close by your expensive supermarket, you would likely switch stores as in equation (2) because the switching costs are reduced such that the value propositions have changed comparative positions.

As economic conditions deteriorate, the perceived switching costs take on different weightings: the value of the price differential increases in importance relative to the value of time and effort.

Relying on behavioral loyalty in tough economic times is a high-risk strategy. This is particularly the case in mature markets. In these markets, differentiation among competitive products is low and thus behavioral loyalty is highly likely. Moving toward a more sustainable competitive advantage requires the development of the next level of loyalty: cognitive loyalty. This is particularly important in depressed economies.

Cognitive loyalty is a form of loyalty that is unrelated to switching costs. It is purely the relationship between the business and the customer. When cognitive loyalty is achieved, the supplied value proposition (which is closely related to customer satisfaction) is relatively higher to a business's competitors. A high customer satisfaction or net promoter score index might reflect superior product features (tangible and intangible) and will then likely reflect an increase in the perception of value the customer feels they are receiving.

Repeated satisfaction typically leads to increased trust. Historically earned trust can supplant a consumer's need for a certain level of additional information. In other words, if a consumer has trust, they will require less information than if they don't have trust. In a hard economic environment, a consumer will rely more on trust yet will also slightly increase their need for additional information.

Regarding the economies of trust, when a consumer trusts a business, it costs the business less in acquisition costs and also less in servicing costs. This is because customers require less of the business to convince them of the business's superior value relative to competitors. These trust economics are a trust annuity over time: the more trust, the more sustainable competitive advantage. Thus, cognitive loyalty is the most sustainable form of loyalty. Businesses entering a recession or economic downturn with cognitive loyalty will have a better chance of retaining their customers than those businesses with simply behavioral loyalty.*

Four central types of loyalty

Within the two categories of loyalty, there are four essential types of loyalty. Each of these has its own benefits, risks, and measurement needs.

1. **Contractual loyalty.** When a customer buys through an official agreement, you have contractual loyalty. This is typical for B2B transactions. The DuPont example represents contractual loyalty. Contractual loyalty also applies to consumer situations like subscriptions for newspapers and magazines, or for cable, telephone, or web services.

    Contractual loyalty can be highly profitable when looked at from a net present value perspective. But it is less profitable as contracts are renegotiated and competitors can use aggressive tactics to steal your customers during these times. Contractual loyalty can also create dissatisfaction. Customers may feel trapped in a business contract. Dell uses its key account program, Premier.Dell.com, to add value to the traditional contracts by allowing business buyers to place their orders online 24/7.

2. **Transactional loyalty.** Repeat purchasing without any contractual responsibility is termed transactional loyalty:

*Source: Peter Niemeyer.

The customer is in the market for a certain type of widget and you sell widgets. Loyalty is based on dimensions such as price, value perception, and convenience. The customer may find a better deal at any time and switch without hesitation.

The doctor writing prescriptions for Pfizer drugs is an example of transactional loyalty. She writes one prescription at a time. Because the doctor's loyalty is affected by her medical assessment – the product costs her nothing, and she gets an occasional free trip each year – the economic relationship is vulnerable to a better deal, e.g. more free trips. If some other pharmaceutical manufacturer develops a better educational program in a more attractive warm weather location, it is likely the physician will prescribe equivalent products from the new company offering the better perks.

Transactional loyalty is easy to stimulate with promotions or rewards programs. But to the degree nonessential promotional elements are used, "loyalty" can be difficult to sustain at a profitable level. In addition, transactional loyalty can be achieved primarily from a customer's perception of the switching cost relative to moving their business. With financial services, consumers may perceive a great deal of work in switching banks for slightly higher value propositions.

3. **Functional loyalty.** To the functionally loyal customer, the product's core attributes are perceived as superior, thus more desirable. One wireless phone company may provide superior reception at the customer's home, making for solid functional loyalty. The Nike example represents functional loyalty; if you have wide feet, you develop a functional loyalty to footwear that fits your large feet.

Functional loyalty is often the first loyalty strategy of businesses to create differentiation. To the degree that you can offer customers product features that are tangible and relevant to the category purchase, you can secure that portion of the market that prioritizes your advantaged product feature.

4. **Emotional loyalty.** This is the human side or the "feeling" part of loyalty, in which a customer develops preferences for products or services based on their appeal to the individual's higher order emotions, e.g. values, ego, sensibilities. Customers identify with the brand, like the traveler searching for a Starbucks, because they seek some higher order benefit that represents little or no functional value to them by association. It is more about the high order experience. Emotional loyalty is the Holy Grail for most businesses – most seek this type of loyalty but few achieve it.

One of the primary pluses of emotional loyalty is its ability to withstand challenge during changes in economic cycles or service relationships: Emotionally loyal customers will forgive minor errors in their experience and maintain their loyalty. Also, emotional loyalty is often associated with price premiums in household brands that have no noticeable differences in form, function, value, or convenience.*

As Figure 4.1 depicts, behavioral and transactional loyalty are the most prevalent types of loyalty. These two types are adequate for strong economies. Once the economy has started deteriorating, they have little or no lasting value. The more sustainable types of loyalty, e.g. functional, cognitive,

*Source: Stuart Ayling.

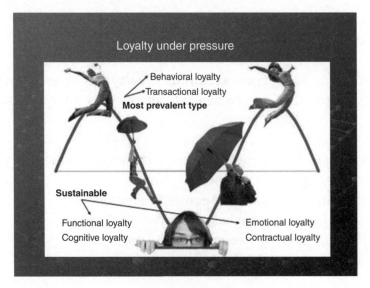

Figure 4.1

emotional, and contractual, will sustain through contracted economies.

As with the basic management tenet, what gets measured gets done – loyalty needs to be measured. Each kind of loyalty – contractual, transactional, emotional, and functional – is open to its own set of metrics.

Because **contractually loyal** customers are buying under a purchase agreement, the agreement and its status need to be measured. Ways to do this include:

- share of market under contract;
- frequency distribution of contract profitability;
- frequency distribution of customer share of wallet;
- contract renewal rates (perhaps by inception date cohorts);
- incidence of contract expansion into new product lines or business units;

- customer referral frequency;
- effective price changes at renewal.

Customers with **transactional loyalty** are characterized by patterns that can be teased out by data analytics, such as:

- changes in recency-frequency-monetary value by customer segment or cohort group;
- velocity of change in segment mobility;
- cross-category purchase behavior and trends;
- latency (gaps between transactions);
- frequency distribution of transaction value.

With the **functionally loyal** buyer, the key is to closely monitor the basis of the functional preference. Measurement approaches include:

- top-of-mind awareness on key functional dimensions;
- changes in perceptions of key functional attributes vs. those of competitors;
- willingness to recommend;
- price elasticity.

Measuring **emotional loyalty** involves:

- attitudinal surveys on key attributes;
  - "like me",
  - "a brand I can trust",
  - "the right brand for the times";
- competitive brand preference;
- price insensitivity;
- problem tolerance;
- resistance to competitive offers;
- overall brand preference.

The key to loyalty measurement effectiveness is to have a very clear picture of the economic value you are trying to create. If there is no expectation of superior economic value in either the short or long term, then initiatives intended to inspire customer loyalty can't possibly pass the basic business-case test.

The business case for loyalty

For most businesses, the promise of customer loyalty implies potential economic value creation with some combination of the following five dimensions.

First, many companies invest in an unbalanced fashion in *customer acquisition* activities – particularly at the beginning of their relationship. This places them in an unprofitable situation from the start. The strategy is to pay off the initial investment many times over during the lifetime of their customer relationship.

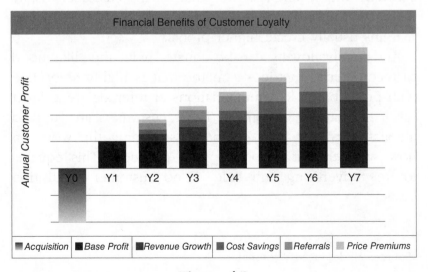

Figure 4.2

Second, loyal customers are inclined to buy more products and a broader array of products. This creates a higher return over the life of the customer relationship. Estimate how much these customers spend with you over their lifetimes, and arrive at the financial benefit.

Third, loyalty can be a *strategy for reducing ongoing expense*. A business that is retaining customers will be required to invest less per customer relative to acquiring a new customer. By patching the "hole in the bottom of the customer bucket" businesses can also stave off the drain of financial resources required to acquire new customers in a very competitive marketplace. This was illustrated by Frederick Reichheld in his breakthrough 1996 study, *The Loyalty Effect*. It analyzed the bottom-line value of an additional five percentage points in retention rate across a variety of industries. Competition in most industries is unrelenting. Customers are intrinsically not loyal. The more attractive and relevant your customer value proposition is, the less likely they are to defect to your competitor.

Fourth, customer loyalty is directly related to a *lower price elasticity* and willingness on behalf of the customer to pay more for the "privilege" of buying your products. Higher margins usually create higher profits.

And finally, loyalty can be equated with the "likelihood to recommend" metric – a metric that is highly associated with profitability. Recommendations or referrals are a direct result of "happy" customers. These customers are "unpaid ambassadors" for your company, spreading the word on how wonderful it is to buy your products. This equates to free advertising and little or no customer acquisition costs.*

*Source: MarketingNPV Journal.

Case study: Suncorp Metway

A large bank and insurance company in Australia with assets of over $31 billion, and 3.5 million customers began their journey by first understanding what customers perceived as having relative value.

Making the assumption that consumers are totally economically driven in tough economies is not necessarily correct. While consumers have a heightened sensitivity for price, they are also making more fear-based decisions and want to know that their bank or insurance company will be there for them in troubled times. Thus, Suncorp Metway made the decision not to move into a discounting position. This was to protect against runaway commoditization of their products and to retain their trust levels with consumers, i.e. "if you're discounting products now, can I still trust you in these hard times for the level of service I still need?"

Suncorp Metway researched their marketplace and found that none of their competitors is considered exceptional in delivering customer service. In effect, the competitive positioning labeled "top notch services" was vacant. One of the main factors behind the widespread consumer perception of lowered service levels in the Australian financial services marketplace is that in the mid 80s, all of Suncorp Metway's large bank competitors were faced with downsizing their massive branch infrastructure because of the overwhelming expense burden in another tough economy. In doing this, they undertook large-scale branch closures, which directly impacted many small towns and suburban centers. At these locations, branches were replaced by automated service options such as ATMs and telephone banking. While the reaction to this tough economy kept them shoring up expenses, it created tremendous animosity with customers, to the point that derogatory comments about the eroding quality of bank services became commonplace, both in the media and in political circles. This new Australian "sport" was – and still is – colloquially known as "bank bashing". At the same time, most of Suncorp Metway's competitors implemented aggressive "fee for service" initiatives because of increasing expense pressures.

In the previous banking era, many of the service levels had been cross-subsidized by other profitable segments of the business. As those very profitable segments dwindled, the big banks seemed to have little choice but to reduce levels of service to their customers. For example, when a customer had funds in a checking account, which earned no interest, the banks could use the money to fund services in another area of the bank. In today's banking model, the banks are charging a fee for each service. The most widely resented fees are from ATM charges and competitors' ATM charges. Customers have reacted negatively to this "death by a 1000 cuts" approach – seen as reducing levels of customer service while introducing a range of new or increasing fees. In today's tough economy, consumers are hypersensitive to this type of fee strategy.

Suncorp Metway also has the advantage of being perceived as a "regional" bank rather than one of the "Big 4" which immediately gives it an added perception of a safe haven with a high level of service. This perception is also fueled by the local press publicizing issues of social responsibility for banks in small towns and suburban locations.

To understand what the consumers "valued" relative to their competition, they started implementing their "worth what you pay for" approach by bringing together all the "stakeholders" of all the seven major lines of business. These seven lines of business are broadly grouped into one of four areas – consumer banking, investments, insurance, and business banking.

Consumer banking includes transaction banking and home lending. Business banking includes owner-managed businesses, and small to medium-sized businesses. Insurance includes home insurance and motor insurance. These seven main lines of business accounted for over 80% of Suncorp Metway's revenue. This made it critically important for Suncorp Metway to undertake specific service initiatives in each of these areas to differentiate their levels of service from their competitors. They refer to these specific service initiatives as their "Blue Ribbon" service initiatives.

Based on the current economic conditions, and now understanding their relative value proposition, they built their business case and then communicated. They launched the first group of five Blue Ribbon initiatives. The business case they built for the consumer was:

1. Simple
2. Relative
3. Quantified

Blue Ribbon initiatives

- Home Loans – qualified approvals by phone in less than 15 minutes.
- Call Center Hold time 60 seconds or less.
- Motor insurance repairs within five days.
- Business Loan approval within five days.
- Branch teller queues wait times five minutes or less.

Both groups of consumers (Inerts and Hunters) responded well to this.

The common tag line across their ads is "Remember service?" "We do".The danger in downturn economies is that price cutting is the first reaction. In this case, from their research they found that if they were competitive, service was still highly valued by their customers.

Here are the first five Blue Ribbon service initiatives in more detail.

1. **Home Loans – qualified approvals by phone in less then 15 minutes.** Suncorp Metway's home loans Blue Ribbon initiative promises that if a customer calls Suncorp Metway on the phone for a home loan, they will con- organization how much the customer can borrow within 15 minutes. Suncorp Metway will also provide a personal home loan consultant to meet personally with the customer at the customer's convenience to help design the ideal home loan solution. The promise reads as follows "Call Suncorp Metway for a home loan and we'll con- organization how much you can borrow within 15 minutes. We'll also provide your own personal home loan consultant who'll meet with you on your terms to help design the ideal home loan solution."

2. **Call Center Hold time 60 seconds or less.** Suncorp Metway's research revealed that Australian banks – as well as many other large organizations – had unwittingly fomented a deep undercurrent of resentment amongst consumers by introducing "automated" phone services that downplayed or discouraged the human factor. These phone systems are designed so that customers are forced to step through numerous menu options before being able to choose to speak to a real human. Even after selecting the option to talk to a human being, customers are often placed on "hold" while waiting to speak to the next available consultant. Typically, the hold time is filled with automated recordings repeating messages along the lines of "Your call is very important to us …". What most companies don't realize is that poorly worded

messages such as "Your call is very important to us ..." can have the opposite effect to that intended and can actually create distrust because the company itself is proving by its action that the customer is not especially important to them since the customer is forced to languish on hold while listening through many iterations of these recordings. Essentially, it is proof that the company is hypocritical and not truthful. Not a good way to kick off any genuinely important human conversation. In addition, the company often doesn't have the competency to support these words in any other fashion.

When Suncorp Metway analyzed the key drivers of the overall telephone banking experience, the negative consequences of forcing customers to navigate voice response systems (VRS) without any immediate option to talk to a real human became clear. The analysis also revealed that most customers in this day and age are reasonably willing to accept that sometimes a short wait on hold may be needed. But, when hold times exceed a maximum threshold, customers' acceptance drops away dramatically, as their sensation of feeling like "just another account number" in a dehumanized process overshadows the rest of the service encounter. The result is a customer who is dissatisfied with the overall experience. When the dehumanization of the voice response systems is coupled with other partially dehumanizing interactions (e.g. "can you please tell me your 10 digit account number?") the cumulative buildup creates a lasting negative image in the customer's mind that is not easily overcome. In order for a organization to overcome a series of negative human interactions, it would have to perfectly execute at least four largely positive humanizing interactions sequentially to change a negative overall impression.

Suncorp Metway found that they could accurately predict their customer satisfaction score based on the elapsed time it took for a customer to speak to a real human customer support person. They also could accurately predict how long a customer was willing to wait on hold without significantly impacting the satisfaction of the call. They found that the customer's tolerance for waiting on hold dramatically falls after roughly 60 seconds. From this analysis, Suncorp Metway set a target of answering 9 out of 10 customers (90%) who wanted to talk to a real human in 60 seconds or less. Once they consistently achieved this level of competency, they began a public advertising campaign based on this service standard under the banner of their Blue Ribbon initiatives. In addition, the remaining 1 out of 10 customers do not wait much longer than 60 seconds. Operationally, implementing this type of competency required certain shifts in staffing as well as the appropriate training for the staff and the right tools, e.g. scripts. This "60 seconds or less" Blue Ribbon initiative was advertised along with four similar Blue Ribbon initiatives. Suncorp Metway's promise reads as follows: "We aim to ensure most telephone calls to our call center are answered in under one minute. Already, we answer 90% of calls in under 60 seconds."

3. **Motor insurance repairs within five days.** From their CVA research, Suncorp Metway realized that the reputation of many car insurers was quite poor when it came to the process of actually lodging a claim and getting a damaged vehicle repaired quickly and competently. This offered a tremendous opportunity to differentiate themselves in service levels. Suncorp Metway began by instituting its own assessment centers, which created a foundation for removing many of the dehumanizing elements from the auto claims process. Suncorp

Metway discovered that much of the human anxiety that plagues customers who need to process auto claims comes in the form of the following uncertainties:

- How long is my car going to be off the road?
- What hassles do I have to go through to get my car fixed?
- Do I have to get three different written quotes from three different repairers?
- How do I know that the repairer is going to give me a quality job?

In addition, most customers only have a minimal understanding of how automobiles function, and have no real desire to ever learn – they simply want their car to work. To be thrust into a situation where an unknown party (repairer) is dealing with their automobile, the level of uncertainty and human anxiety climbs to an even higher level. From these human behavioral discoveries, Suncorp Metway has created a Blue Ribbon initiative promising their customer that if their car is still drivable after an accident (80% are still drivable), the customer only needs to drive their car to any one of Suncorp Metway's assessment centers, which are located in every major city in Queensland. Suncorp Metway will then repair the car and guarantee the repairs for life. These repairs are promised to be completed within seven days once the car is dropped off. If for whatever reason the repairs take longer than seven days, Suncorp Metway will provide their customer a courtesy car at no charge. Suncorp Metway found from their survey research that one of the factors that drives much of the dissatisfaction in the auto claims process is the anxiety that the customer is going to get "screwed" by the insurer or repair facility.

Recognizing this, Suncorp Metway has designed their ads to address the common anxieties and cynicism of customers going through the auto claims process. Looking at their consolidated research across a range of service encounters and market sectors, Suncorp Metway concluded that a constantly recurring factor causing the buildup of human anxiety in any service encounter is driven by the time pressure placed on most customers' lives. This is why many of Suncorp Metway's service initiatives are linked to giving back time to the customer. They are careful to communicate that customers can confidently expect quite specific and predictable time savings when they choose to interact with Suncorp Metway. More importantly, before any advertising of the time savings occurs, Suncorp Metway makes sure they can operationally deliver on their promise consistently. Thus, for the car repair initiative, Suncorp Metway's promise reads as follows: "If you're able to drive your Suncorp Metway insured car into one of our assessment centers in South East Queensland after an approved claim, we'll have you back on the road within a week. All repair work will be guaranteed for life. And if for some reason we can't fix your car within 7 days we'll arrange a free courtesy car for you until your car is repaired."

When Suncorp Metway initially investigated the emotional dimensions in a typical customer's insurance claim, they discovered that most customers were under growing time constraints in their normal lives. For these customers, any event or activity placing increased potential pressure – imagined or real – on this time constraint caused a significant increase in their anxiety level. From this early information, Suncorp Metway began focusing on the cycle time of the end-to-end insurance claim process. As they investigated further into the emotional aspects of the customer's perception of the overall experience, they found that there was a series of activities, or lack of activities, beyond the time issue that left customers with "nagging" doubts as to whether they were truly being taken care of by Suncorp Metway. Much of this customer anxiety seemed to form the spontaneous starting point for each individual, fed by years of negative word-of-mouth about banks and insurance companies, and their impersonal and dehumanizing manners. The result is an ambient background noise or legacy of customer distrust, which functions as a fertile breeding ground for suspicion and fears of somehow being tricked. It was common to have a customer's lack of trust breed thoughts such as "There must be some tiny loophole that they are going to use to cheat me".

This legacy of distrust, along with the customers' time constraints, led Suncorp Metway to focus on providing a quick turnaround for the customers' auto claims while leaving the customer in no doubt that their car would be properly repaired with high-quality parts and craftsmanship. An important lesson for Suncorp Metway to learn was that even though they had operationally already addressed this legacy of distrust by providing a lifetime guarantee on the repairs, they had previously failed to adequately communicate this to the customers, so that many customers did not realize that this guarantee applied. A promise inadequately communicated to the customer doesn't exist in the minds of the customer. Suncorp Metway discovered this communications issue after it applied high-level statistical analysis to its surveys. It analyzed several of the statistical patterns and delved into the statistical suggestions of this problem with additional focus groups. They also investigated how to best communicate this guarantee to the customer so that they would be most likely to emotionally accept it and understand it. Suncorp Metway found that until they effectively communicated this quality of work guarantee, the customer continued to have doubts as to whether their insurer would really stand behind the repair work.

Another important human need which emerged from additional qualitative work around accident claims was the fact that customers just wanted Suncorp Metway to handle all the "hassles" from the minute the accident happened to when they picked up the car. An auto accident can be a dramatic event. Any entity that can lessen some of the burden arising from that event will garner favor with the customer. As with the lifetime guarantee of quality work, Suncorp Metway had already operationally set up processes to handle all the "hassles" of the claims process for the customer. But, again, they had not adequately communicated this competency and its value to the customers and to the overall marketplace. This prompted Suncorp Metway to be more explicit in communicating how they handle "all the little details" of the claim process and how that benefits the customer emotionally, i.e. "Yes, you will get your car back in seven days, and yes, your repairs will be guaranteed for life, and yes – the actual process is hassle free because all you do is drop your car off at one of our assessment centers and everything else is taken care of by us – you don't have to even think about it until you get your car back."

One of the key aspects of this communication is that it was accomplished with everyday language for real, genuine, ordinary people as opposed to business jargon. While it is very important to use more advanced statistical analysis and survey techniques, many of the clues to the importance of using everyday language came from qualitative focus group observation and from unsolicited customer letters. For example, Suncorp Metway received one letter describing exactly how the customer emotionally felt about each part of their motor claims insurance process. Letters such as these were used to form the communication scripts to describe the total experience of their offerings in this marketplace. Suncorp Metway experimented with applying multiple wordings and intonations to communicate the same simple sentences in order to test the customer's understanding of each idea. Unlike the intent of many common marketing pieces today to manipulate the truth, Suncorp Metway's focus was to clearly articulate the value of its product and services to its customers. Another important issue in communicating Suncorp Metway's value to customers and the marketplace was striving to differentiate their very specific market offerings from their competitors' offerings, which could easily sound very similar. Suncorp Metway found that a powerful way to achieve this was to use a certain level of specificity, clearly delineating their quantifiable service offering from their competitors' "feel good" promises. By being "up front" and specific, and quoting a numeric measure that customers can easily relate to, they could achieve measurable differentiation in the mind of the customer, e.g. seven-day turnaround, 60-second response time.

4. **Business Loan approval within five days.** Suncorp Metway has applied these principles across all their main lines of business, including business banking. For business banking customers, Suncorp Metway's promise reads as follows: "Call Suncorp Metway for a Business Loan and we'll give you an answer, in writing, within 5 working days." This is based on their CVA survey and focus group research conorganizationing that customers in the business sector do value a quick turnaround period for business loans.

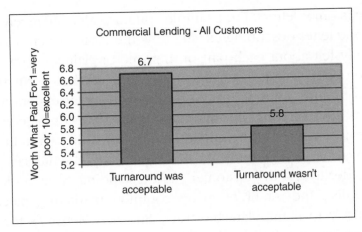

Figure 4.3

The example shown is for the commercial lending market. Figure 4.3 illustrates that customers who experience acceptable turnarounds give higher overall satisfaction ratings.

Figure 4.4 illustrates that acceptability of turnaround time drops quickly beyond a five-day turnaround period.

5. **Branch teller queues wait times five minutes or less.** In its bank branches, Suncorp Metway has published a service promise whereby a customer will not have to wait more than five minutes in a queue before being served by a consultant. This is referred to as Suncorp Metway's "five-minute" guarantee. Suncorp Metway has chosen this service attribute because their analysis revealed that this was by far the worst performing attribute of a customer's branch service encounter, for all competitors in the industry. In effect, it was a customer "hot button". Across the banking sector, "cost-saving" initiatives over many years have either implicitly or explicitly "pushed" customers away from "expensive" real human beings and toward machine oriented interac-

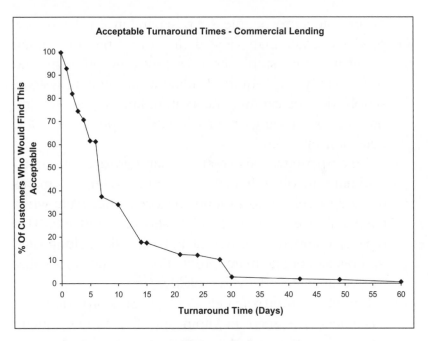

Figure 4.4

tions, e.g. telephone banking and ATMs. While high-level measures of productivity and cost, such as cost-to-income ratios, have been trending downwards for most competitors throughout this same timeframe, the overall gains in productivity have arguably not been as dramatic as might have been expected. One possible reason is that eroding levels of customer satisfaction – which are clearly evident over the last five to 10 years for most of the major competitors in this industry – have had the unintended consequence of increasing other types of costs that are rarely, if ever, captured explicitly in traditional accounting systems. These costs include the cost of increased customer attrition – the "churn" of old customers defecting and needing to be replaced by a similar number of new customers, or the lowering efficiency of sales, as eroding levels of customer loyalty mean that more people shop separately for each new product, rather than view their current provider as an automatic "one stop" shop for any new products and services they may require. Traditional accounting systems simply do not capture the bottom-line impacts of improving or eroding cross-sell rates, repurchase rates, defection rates, etc.

Suncorp Metway also realizes that there are substantial lead times involved in making the process improvements needed to deliver consistently and cost-effectively while maintaining exceptionally high service standards. This type of competitive differentiator can take a long time to replicate, unlike many product-based innovations that can be imitated relatively quickly.

Currently, approximately 95% of Suncorp Metway's customers are served within the five-minute queue waiting time. Suncorp Metway's promise reads as follows: "We aim to serve customers who visit our branches within 5 minutes. Already, 95% of customers are served within this time."

Suncorp Metway's business case approach was successful because they did not assume their customers were emotionally loyal, they did not guess about what consumers valued most, and they did not take their customers' trust for granted. They began by understanding what they valued most relative to their competitors. They honored the trust and loyalty they had and designed their initiatives to build on that. They then crafted the communication of the business case in simple, relative, and quantifiable terms to serve both the Inert and Hunter groups of consumers.

5   B2C Approaches for Dynamic Consumer Needs/Value Tradeoff

Addressing the dynamics of how consumers dynamically change their prioritization of high and low-order needs with the ever evolving mechanics of how they perceive value, each type of economy and transition requires unique approaches. This chapter divides those approaches into three categories – downturn economic cycles, economic transitions, and boom economies.

Approaches for downturn economic cycles

Reframing your competitive set

A drastic change in the economic cycle – be it in a boom or a bust – presents companies with a marketing opportunity. It is the perfect time to reframe or redefine their value proposition. This is also an excellent step in recession-proofing a brand.

Consider the Kool-Aid brand. Many marketers, when evaluating the Kool-Aid competitive set, would include Crystal Light, Tang, generic brands, and juice brands. How many would include soda? To a consumer, they are all options that quench thirst.

During the recent downturn, the price of a case of soda shot way, way up. That's an opportunity. The wise people at Kraft realized that and are reframing the competitive set for Kool-Aid. The repositioned brand will be focusing on its low price: one-third that of soda.

Recession-proofing your brand

There are three things that can help a brand survive changing economic conditions:

1. Redefining what perceived value means
2. Maintaining better product performance
3. Being unique in the marketplace.

With regards to redefining what perceived value means consider Mission Foods. Mission Foods makes tortillas, wraps, taco shells, and chips. But it has recognized that they were not in the food business; rather, they were in the meal solutions business. It delivers value to hungry families, not by just being priced right but by giving families the tools they need to save time in the kitchen. By providing recipes, and cooking tips, Mission Foods delivers value by saving families time, which is often a scarcer commodity than money.

Kellogg's redefine their value proposition by representing themselves as a more economical way to start your family's day: "… it takes just 50 cents a bowl, including milk, to start your family's day with what matters most – a nutritious breakfast together".

Consider Craftsman tools and its lifetime replacement guarantee for their tools. The focus is clearly to provide a better performing product over the lifetime use of that product. When a consumer buys a Craftsman product, the company justifies that the product is worth paying more for because of the guarantee it comes with, thereby giving it a higher perceived value.

Being unique in the marketplace "creates" its own market. Despite cutting back in more upscale product purchases, many consumers are saving so that they can indulge in unique experiences and more luxurious products.

Target Stores launched a compelling viral marketing video on YouTube that reframes their brand and products to a more economical value proposition. The theme of the upbeat video was "a new day ... new ways to save".

The new commute – Bike $59.99
The new gym – Gym ball $11.88
The new movie night – DVD $13.00
The new barber shop – Clippers $14.99
The new family room – Tent $70.49.

The Apple iPhone is an example of this. On July 14, Apple announced that it sold its one-millionth iPhone 3G, just three days after its launch. By comparison, it took 74 days to sell one million iPhones following the initial launch of the product in 2007 and almost two years to achieve the incredible milestone with iPod. The advance information of the iPhone 3G had successfully convinced consumers the product was unique. The prevailing economic cycle had little relevancy.*

To adjust or not adjust pricing

A business must first assess its brand position and understand the dynamics of a down economy and whether it is a smart, long-term decision to adjust pricing.

*Source: Nicole Granese.

If a business had a high-end product and decided to boost sales with a discount strategy, consumers would translate that into lower quality and instead of buying the high-quality product, they would possibly decide not to buy it because of what the lower price implied in terms of quality and even status, i.e. classic brand erosion. There is a huge risk in shifting a value proposition too far away from its origins. It's very easy to see an erosion in the brand.

For example: R.M. Williams knows that boots can't just look good. They have to fit comfortably as well. From the first moment, they should feel like your feet have known them for years. R.M. Williams have more sizes than most boot makers (and they fit where it counts). The price is high: $300 or $400. It might be considered overpriced but it's also what customers have come to expect. If R.M. Williams started offering value-based boots for 70 ready dollars, what would be customers' reactions? Many wouldn't even look at the brand. They're known as a prestige brand. If they start to discount and offer an alternative pricing option, customers will question the brand credibility based on what has been established over time. Trust, the all-important trust, will have been compromised.

Focus marketing initiatives in sync with consumers'/customers' source of funding

One of the critical elements of successfully navigating economic cycles is to focus marketing initiatives in line with how consumers/customers change how they fund purchases. In the airline industry, downturns in economic conditions have a significant change in both their business and leisure markets. In the business travel market, all of the travel is funded by the employees' business, which makes it critical to track the changes in corporate policy. In the leisure travel market, consumers fund their travel with either cash or credit. For the American consumer, it is predominately credit, which is fueled by the availability of credit. This credit is particularly driven by equity in the housing markets. Therefore it is important to track not only the credit markets but also the housing market.

In economic downturns, typically businesses curtail overall business travel as well as change policies relative to flying first or business class. As economic cycles get worse, many may institute moratoriums on travel, which significantly impact the airline industry. In such cases, business demand cannot be stimulated by traditional levers. Changing pricing strategy would do little or no good if businesses stop using business or first class travel completely. Therefore, the industry has to understand corporate pricing policy changes and the timing of those changes relative to economic cycles.

In the airline industry, premium business travel is the first segment to soften. This softening then extends to the broader business travel market. The next area is a broader softening of business travel demand. In this case, airlines typically have to just "wait it out" until businesses free up funding for premium business travel.

In the leisure travel market, airlines can typically still apply different pricing strategies to affect demand. While business travel is completely driven by corporate edict, leisure travel is driven by discretionary income. Therefore, the airline industry must understand what the source of funds of discretionary income is for their customers. This varies by factors such as geographic region and socioeconomic segment.

While the leisure travel market still has responsiveness to changing pricing strategies in downturn economies, there continues to be a tradeoff between achieving a higher load factor on the airplanes (industry's measure of occupancy) and degradation in the brand because of discounting. This balance can be best achieved by applying price sensitivity algorithms and opinion surveys on the discounting strategy.

Recession marketing

The 2008 meltdown which can also be known as the current perfect storm comes to us with two economic "storm fronts".

1. Most organizations have lagged behind their investments in interactive media and well behind consumer's adoption rates.

2. We have had a fundamental shift in the consumer environment – from abundant to scary.

Both marketing dimensions must be addressed now … Not tomorrow, not next week, now. The consumer is in survival mode and so is your business. Your business will not survive these scary times without:

* creating an edict of acute listening to the consumer's changing needs;
* transparent collaboration and participating in THEIR survival of the scary times;
* bringing them generous and genuine value.

Do these three things and you will go beyond survival to significance in their eyes.

Now is the perfect time to advertise!

Media prices have been lowered and you'll stand out above your competitors and show consumers that you are strong enough to advertise and weather this downturn. The key is to craft messages that reflect the times and show how your service or product is worth the consumer's dollars; advertising is an investment, not an extraneous expense. We still need food, transportation, shelter, things to put in our homes, etc. ... As Americans it is ingrained in our souls to consume. I doubt any American has completely cut out buying things they "don't need" to save money. Have they slimmed down their spending? Absolutely. Have they cut out nonessential expenses altogether? Absolutely not. Here are some examples.

The dairy industry hired personal finance guru Suze Orman to champion milk as a bargain (see Figure 5.1). It's just one example of "recession marketing" – urging people to buy merchandise that saves them money.

Figure 5.1

Allstate insurance is meeting hard times head on. In one TV spot, featuring the reassuring actor Dennis Haysbert (perhaps best known as President David Palmer on the Fox drama "24"), the company reminds viewers that it got its start in 1931, during the Great Depression. "And through the 12 recessions since," Haysbert says, Allstate has noticed that "after the fears subside, a funny thing happens: People start enjoying the small things in life. It's back to basics, and the basics are good." Home and auto insurance, apparently, are among the basics.

Hyundai, the Korean auto manufacturer, is running an ad in which the voiceover intones: "Buy any new Hyundai and if in the next year you lose your income, we'll let you return it." Because, the ad continues, "We're all in this together. And we'll all get through it together."

Additionally, Hyundai started a new program that allows buyers to return the cars for free if they lose their job or lose their driver's license due to medical reasons. Tom Hollett of Huffines Hyundai says "Losing your job involuntarily is a big one that I know a lot of people are concerned about."

The program was available for one year on all remaining 2008 and new 2009 models. Since every new customer qualified, Hyundai hoped it would convince people to sign on the dotted line. Tom Hollett says "They're looking for a good product and a good warranty, and something that gives them good peace of mind that the product they own at a fair payment is going to deliver."

Teri Everett says "I think this is very good for people in this slower economy. Because a lot of people are losing their job and getting laid off, and it's good to know that you have the assurance that your car will be taken care of if you can't afford it."*

*Source: Linton Weeks.

Manage discounting

As many businesses find themselves in contracting economies, they decide to discount heavily to maintain revenue
levels. This must always be done in concert with the realiza-
tion that brand damage is possible. If the business decides
that the brand can sustain the impact of heavy discounting,
this can be a valid marketing approach – but be careful.

Plan pricing strategy scenarios in advance of transitions
and stick to them. Economic cycles take the full range of
depth and duration. They are difficult to predict at best.
Many businesses find themselves in reactionary modes and
making business decisions that are based on fear, which
many times lead to long-term damage. It is best to create
pricing strategy scenarios before an economy's transition
either up or down. This is helpful in taking the "emotion"
out of the moment.

In 2008, the Christmas season demonstrated many examples of retail businesses taking a wide range of pricing
strategies. For some, it was all about protecting margins
and the brand. For others, it was pure volume. For the
high-end retailer Abercrombie and Fitch, the CEO was
adamant that they would not discount during the holiday
season to both protect margins and ultimately their brand
of being an exclusive retailer. One could walk through
different shopping malls and see the proliferation of sale
layered on sale advertisements. The Abercrombie and
Fitch's storefront was conspicuously absent of any sale sign
– even during the competitive Christmas season. This was
clearly a statement to their customers that they still represent the highest quality and most exclusive clothing choice
and their pricing would still reflect that pricing power.
Abercrombie and Fitch volumes did go down as much as
60% but their margins held. One of their closest competitors, J. Crew, another retailer who targets the higher-end

customers, was starting their Christmas season discounts at 50% and adding another 20% discount on top of that for a series of one-day only sales to drive volume with little regard for margin.

For a high-end tour operator, they took a similar approach to protecting not only their margins but their message of a quality product. Their segment was family vacations starting at $10,000 and up. They made the conscious decision not to change pricing whatsoever. A large part of this was sending a message to the marketplace that their product was of high quality and that their prices would continue to reflect that quality. They did have a reasonable reduction in bookings but still the business stayed viable. During the economic contraction, they had to transition from a business growth strategy to a sustainability state strategy which meant scaling down organizationally. All of their moves to create standard sustainability were done with the consciousness of not affecting service levels to their guests.

Even some high-quality retailers come to the fear in the retail marketplace. Nordstrom was a retailer with a long-standing reputation for high quality with major sales events only occurring notably two times a year. They broke this long-standing market position with taking markdowns almost the entire month of December. Saks Fifth Avenue took a similar path in aggressive markdowns starting in the second week in December, e.g. a $600 raincoat for $179. These retailers drove volume with the discounting strategy but likely experienced brand damage because of it.

Pricing strategies are many times determined by underlying infrastructural costs, i.e. what it costs to open the doors every day for destination cities like Las Vegas. Pricing strategies that were in place had little relevance to the severity of the last downturn. Instead of heavily discounting hotel rooms, they were offering rooms free of charge with additional coupons given at check-in for dining and entertainment. Most, if not all, of their pricing strategies were not developed toward such a depth of economic downturn. Typically, in prosperous economies the casinos would be brimming full of people with little room to walk through them. At the bottom of the recession, they were only scattered people through most of the casinos.

Part of the resistance to planning for different economic scenarios is that people as human beings don't like to think about worst-case scenarios. It is important for businesses to work through this to make pricing strategies for every type of economy – before they actually happen.

Addressing media created buying anxiety

For the most part, the Canadian financial institutions weather global economic downturns quite well because of Canada's regulation. In the last downturn, the Canadian media was creating the public sentiment that lending in Canada had significantly decreased. The reality is that the lending by banks in Canada was still as close to the relative capacity as it was before the downturn. Yet consumers were under the impression that lending practices have created a significantly tighter lending environment. As the saying goes, "perception is reality". This consumer perception had a noticeable impact on the volume of lending that a Canadian bank was booking. The local branches had to make a concerted effort to dispel this untruth with facts. This is a relatively common phenomenon when an economy transitions from prosperity to retraction. What sells media is bad news. This is why there needs to be a proactive effort on any business's agenda to explicitly address the media's tendency to paint a darker picture than reality.

Replacing fear with facts

In a contracting economy, fear-based buying (or lack of buying) is not only generated by actual economic conditions but also by the media. Regardless, a successful approach in mitigating some of these fears and anxieties is replacing the fear with facts.

One large wealth management company practiced this approach with their clients. They were able to demonstrate that while the economic conditions of the market world were weak, the historic track record of investing in the stock market still proved to be the most financially sound decision. Peter Lynch, former portfolio manager for the Fidelity Magellan fund, commented: "If the Dow and the overall market fall five to 10%, and you feel compelled to sell, don't invest in the stock market. These drops are normal. They happen every 12 to 15 months and you need to have the stomach to ride them out. If you worry about what the market will do in the next six to 12 months, you are not investing. You are gambling. Some of the best stocks pay off handsomely in three years, some in five. In every case, earnings make the difference." Facts to replace fear.

Tapping the one-time "business survival" sale

Brand integrity is all-important to any business, particularly premium brands. There comes a time in the life cycle of most businesses where driving immediate business activity becomes critical to short-term survival. The question becomes: Will a business survival sale, i.e. "Black Friday" sale, cause damage to a reputable brand? Will this type of sale set the expectation in the customer's minds of a new price point for the brand?

History has shown that one-time sales that are an anomaly to the business model do not affect brand integrity or the consumer expectation of a new price point. One particular high-end automotive wheel manufacturer experienced a radical drop in their ordering the month after a radical downturn in the economy. They faced the critical decision whether to hold a "Black Friday" sale or radically change manufacturing levels and lay off employees. The decision was made to hold a one-time "Black Friday" sale. Their results exceeded anything they had planned for. They expanded brand awareness in the marketplace, created full production runs for the following two months, and received countless thank-yous from grateful customers for now being able to afford their premium wheel. There was little or no animosity with their other customers who had just paid full price because the sale was done explicitly as a one-time only. This type of Black Friday sale only works when it is done as an anomaly in the eyes of the customers.

Keep the honesty and trust level high in tough times

It is the natural reaction for businesses to be more guarded internally and externally in difficult economies. Behaviorally, when human beings are under stress, they are hypersensitive to what they perceive as guarded behavior. This is why being as truthful as possible and communicating that truth as often as possible will keep productive activity high and minimize negative rumors (which are destructive to corporate work environments). This open and truthful environment also keeps the flow of good ideas moving throughout the organization, as typically tougher times tend to constrict innovation.

When one retail executive commented that a supportive and open environment is his priority, particularly when economies contract, he added that it is also critical for a sense of integrity. It is equally as important to keep honesty and trust high with customers.

Hyundai example

The automotive manufacturer Hyundai came out with an advertising campaign that addressed the high anxiety over consumers losing their jobs in tough economic times. Hyundai referred to this campaign as their Assurance Plus program. Hyundai Assurance Plus stated that "[F]or a limited time, if you lose your income, we'll make your payments for three months … if that's not enough time to work things out, you can still bring it back … between April 1 and April 30, get great deals on any car in our full line of fine days … 10-year/100,000 mile powertrain warranty."

They initiated this campaign in a depressed economy while none of their competitors initially offered comparable programs. As a result it was a very successful campaign. The program started April 1 and ran until April 30. The company said the program helped it avoid a potential double-digit sales decline in the month, instead reporting just a 2% slide.

Naturally, Ford Motor Co. and General Motors Corporation followed suit, offering payment protection plans to help reassure consumers who may be putting off buying a new car because of worries about losing their job. The offers came as auto sales reached their lowest levels in 27 years. Ford's program will cover payments of up to $700 each month for up to a year on any new Ford, Lincoln, or Mercury vehicle if the buyer loses their job. GM then said it will make a similar offer making up to nine car payments of $500 each for customers who have lost their jobs through no fault of their own. Customers must qualify for state unemployment to be eligible for the program.

While the competition follow suit, trust and honesty points go to the first one out of the box. Customers could see that Hyundai did it voluntarily; Ford and GM did it "because they had to".

Counteracting learned helplessness

Contracting and recession economies create and encourage learned helplessness. Learned helplessness as a technical term in animal psychology and related human psychology means a condition of a human being or an animal in which it has learned to behave helplessly, even when the opportunity is restored for it to help itself by avoiding an unpleasant or harmful circumstance to which it has been subjected. Learned helplessness theory is the view that clinical depression and related mental illnesses result from a perceived absence of control over the outcome of a situation (Seligman, 1975). Approaches to overcome learned helplessness is to create products and services that create self-help market niches in addition to regular markets in prospering economies.

One particular Canadian province was overrun by applications for unemployment insurance. The way they dealt with this was to offer "self-help" seminars. These were focused on the consumer segments that contained learned helplessness. This not only alleviated much of the angst in applying for unemployment insurance but also gave the citizens a sense of empowerment in place of their sense of helplessness.

Focus on "what customers do", not "what they say they'll do" relative to price sensitivity

As economic conditions cycle through their inevitable patterns, businesses need to understand how consumer behavior evolves relative to price sensitivity. It is common to ask customers what they are sensitive to in relation to price changes. Often, however, what they say they are sensitive to and how they behave relative to a price change are two completely different realities.

Although surveying customers regarding their price sensitivities is a common practice, it often leads businesses to create pricing strategies that are inconsistent with their objectives because customers are inconsistent when it comes to what they verbalize their projected behavior will be and how they actually end up behaving.

A major vacation destination company wanted to explore whether their customers would pay a higher price for their destination packages if they bundled ancillary add-ons into the package price, e.g. health club access, local phone calls, bottles of water. One of the motivations behind bundling many of these items was to migrate them away from the "lightning rod" category, as customers were reacting strongly to their unbundled price structure relative to similar items available for much less outside the destination location.

While the customers had said they wanted things more packaged, the reality of them using the cheaper "street" priced products didn't support that. This vacation destination company ended up bundling certain items but keeping other lightning rod items separate with an adjustment on those prices so they were closer to the competing street price. The strong negative reaction of the perceived sizable price difference was not worth the negative effect the additional margin had on the customer experience.

The best approach in determining where the truth lies between what customers say they will do and what they actually will do is to combine test pricing exercises with a balance of pre-survey and actual behavior tracking prior to launching a major pricing strategy change.

Market down – segment

As consumers migrate down the economic retraction slope, consumers migrate their spending away from discretionary spending. The Miller Zell study shows that consumers "trade down" in times of retraction. For example: they shift their dining habits to "eat in" more frequently. The Miller Zell study shows that in periods of recession, 50% of consumers spend less in overall categories. At the same time, 62% of consumers spend the same or more in grocery stores. In an economic recession, general consuming trends across age, gender, and income reflect reduced spending and movement to trading down. 87% of consumers switched to private label brands. 68% of consumers decided to stay home versus dining out. Five out of 10 consumers had brought back special occasions or family nights into their routine. Consumers with incomes over $100K were far more negative about the economy than all other income levels.

Great time to expand marketing activities

When employees are less busy, it is a great time to put them to work on additional marketing campaigns tuned for the economy. One Canadian health spa used its less busy time to expand its email promotions. It put much of its operational staff toward additional marketing efforts to promote coupons and discounts based on a limited time offer.

Leverage consumers' increased free time

During contracted economies, consumers have more free time because of such factors as decreased discretionary money and increased unemployment. Depending on your particular business, it is worth exploring what products and services are more dependent on a consumer's discretionary time. In such service industries as the legal profession and wealth management organizations, many consumers postpone such activities because they require an investment of time, which during prosperous periods is at a premium. When economies contract, consumers are less busy in their conventional jobs either because of a business slow down or unemployment. This is a good time to initiate marketing campaigns to capitalize on the increase in free time of consumers. One Canadian law organization initiated a marketing campaign to potential clients to have province-mandated land registration legal changes done at a discount for a limited time. The marketing message was "Come do it now because you going to have to do it anyway and we'll give you a break on it if you do it now." Ordinarily, the law organization would not solicit for this legal business but it was a very effective marketing campaign during a contracted economy. The campaign was very successful.

Help consumers manage what they owe you

One barrier to consumers' purchasing is the fear that they will not be able to pay for it. For businesses that sell large ticket items, including expensive service offerings, a proactive plan should be in place to ease the consumers' fear about how they will pay you.

These fears are not unfounded as these statistics reveal:

47% – worry about losing their job
71% – know someone who lost their job in the past six months
47% – Both high/low income workers fear job loss
65% – worry about paying bills
69% – worry stocks/retirement investments will drop
53% – worry they don't have enough to retire.*

One large law organization noticed a significant increase in the time they spend with a client talking through how the client will pay the legal bills. In such a case, proactive payment plans should be put in place and even advertised to quell this anxiety not only for initial purchases but also for time efficiencies. This law organization structured their retainer fees and the monthly payments specifically for clients in retracting economies. They also reviewed with the client their ability to meet their obligations prior to initiating the legal work. In prosperous economies, this is a common practice for certain industries but not others such as law organizations. When a legal client walked in the door for litigation work, the due diligence of ability to pay was many times assumed. The discussion is not initially focused on the size of the legal bill but the management of the legal bill, e.g. interim payments, size of payments, monthly payments, down payments.

In contracted economies, it is not only a reduction in how much but how often purchases are made. A Canadian spa experienced a slowdown in the frequency of how often their clients would get their hair cut and colored. In a prosperous economy, clients would get their hair cut and colored every

*Source: Consumer Economic Condition.

six weeks religiously. In a contracted economy, clients would still get their haircut every six weeks but extend their coloring to 10 to 12 weeks. To combat this decrease in frequency, this spa initiated an email coupon campaign targeted at driving the frequency back up. This email campaign was doubly effective because it also utilized the employees whose regular work was reduced redirecting their efforts toward marketing activities.

Manage price perception

Many businesses have the challenge of dispelling the perception that their prices are higher relative to competitors than the actual prices. This is a systemic challenge because behavioral science shows that once consumers have created a perception in their mind, they will not actively seek to either validate or disprove it. One vacation destination had this challenge of dispelling a perception that they were more expensive than their competitors. As economies deteriorate, this perception becomes more ardent because the competitive set widens. For example, if a consumer was considering changing their vacation destination in a good economy to another vacation destination at a slightly lower price point, the price perception would be in the normal range. Once economies worsen, consumers turn toward new alternatives such as family reunions and local parks. In tough economies, more powerful branding and advertising is needed to create the spark to deliver compelling heuristics to prompt consumers to actively revisit their price perception. This vacation destination business initiated an "affordability" advertising campaign which effectively prompted consumers to react positively, e.g. "Oh wow?!, Really?!, It's that affordable?!"

Strategies for transition periods

Choose markets that best sustain brand integrity in contracting economies

Economies will perpetually cycle through their contraction/ expansion cycles. Within these economic cycles, there will be certain markets that certain brands are more vulnerable in than others during contracting economies. In a healthy or expanding economy, a high-quality brand may be able to carve out a successful niche in a market that is typically known for its no-frills brand success. As economies contract, this same market may change to the point where the high-quality brand may be unable to sustain itself given the additional economic pressures.

One airline whose primary market was business travelers, i.e. higher brand stature/higher service levels/premium price, also served a market in the US which was predominantly a leisure travel market, i.e. commoditized market/no-frills service level/lowest price. This was a market that was already well served by many low-cost carriers. While the economy was healthy, they could find reasonable success in this market despite the competition being commoditized competitors. As the economy contracted, they were forced to bring their prices more in line with their no-frills competitors as well as charge for services they ordinarily wouldn't. They were also forced to cut service levels. These operational changes were not in line with their brand and its supporting business model.

In addition, this market did not represent extremely high volumes with the redeeming cost economies of scale to help rationalization of that additional fare discounting. With all of these factors juxtaposed to their brand positioning, both their traditional business customers and new no-frills customers were dissatisfied with their attempts to fit this market in a down economy.

Their typical business customers were used to more elegant services from this airline; their no-frills customers could sense that the airline was not optimized for this market. Their employees were also unhappy as they perceived their employer to be a high-quality airline and the low-quality operational changes were unsettling to them. This discomfort was driven by such operational changes as being forced to charge for checked bags on these routes when they normally wouldn't. Other more subtle operational changes were not in sync with their brand stature such as the new egalitarian boarding procedures – atypical for an airline focused on business travelers. This created brand dissidence with their traditional business travelers who viewed this airline as a cut above other airlines. Their operational changes to compete with the "no-frills" pricing and service levels of the commoditized airlines seemed out of place relative to their brand perception.

In contrast: one vacation destination business had chosen markets where even in contracted economies, they could still charge a premium for own-property hotels even though the competing hotels have compellingly competitive service levels.

Gauge capacity expansion/contraction against both competition and satisfaction drivers

As economies contract and expand, businesses must adjust capacity to keep operational costs in line with contracting and expanding revenue levels. One of the capacity challenges for many industries is to balance being efficient in a market while simultaneously ensuring competitive coverage/presence of a market, i.e. be there – be present despite being at operational levels typically deemed as overcapacity. While a contracted economy will naturally take care of some of the competitive necessity for over-capacity to deal with normal market expansions and contractions it will still exist to some extent when competitors are present.

In the airline industry, a particular route may require only two flights to serve it at its highest efficiency level/load capacity but three flights are needed in order to maintain a competitive presence in the third time slot. In a healthy economy, this airline must run three flights regardless of the additional operational cost as a competitive necessity. It's also important in terms of customer satisfaction for customers to have convenient times to arrive at their destinations. Therefore it's important, when making capacity adjustments, to weigh the propensity for customers to opt for competitors' flights with the savings from reducing operational costs.

This is particularly true in the airline industry as is it is one of the most transparent industries with two major competitive decision factors being easily compared: scheduling and price. In addition, one of the key satisfaction drivers in the airline industry is to have flights that are the most convenient for its customers.

Other industries will have different dynamics for both competition and satisfaction drivers. For example, in a vacation destination industry, the dynamics are markedly different in terms of how they manage capacity (schedule and route network) and the related dimensions of customer satisfaction. In one vacation destination business, they could alter the operating hours of certain attractions to compensate for higher or lower demand as long as their customers experienced an average number of rides that created excellent satisfaction scores coupled with other satisfaction dimensions. Unlike the airline industry, once the customers are at the premises, they cannot opt for a competitive alternative. Therefore, operational capacity could be tuned to demand closely.

The retail industry is another industry that can tune their capacity close to their actual demand when economies contract and expand. This should be done by tracking customer behavior and the purchase patterns against all cost points in terms of where they occur, i.e. activity-based costing, and the relative profit contribution. This can only be done when the retailer tracks their sales activity at a detailed level.

Market up – segment

Whether the economy is in a contraction or a recovery, in most product categories, there is a migration of buying up or buying down. When the economy contracts, people make decisions to do like activities or buy like products but seek more economical versions. The same is true of a recovering economy. Many product categories experience buying up which means the consumer is choosing to spend a little more money on a particular product category. When economies are in transition, marketing should be targeted to wherever the consumer's buying trajectory is headed relative to your product offering and relative to your competitors' product offering.

This buying migration occurs in almost every business from restaurants to retail. One example is the case of the restaurant chain Chick-fil-A. They were benefiting from regular customers of restaurants such as Chili's and Fridays because Chick-fil-A's price point was one step down the buying migration stepladder. As the consumers rationalized their eating out activity, they were not willing to give up the experience of eating out but wanted to feel less "guilty" about spending the money in a difficult economy, so buying down was a reasonable alternative. Therefore, businesses' target marketing should be focused not on their current segment but the next consumer segment up, who are in the process of buying down. For recovering economies, the reverse is true. It is also important to apply the same principles to customer retention activities. To do this, businesses need to create marketing messages that promote affordability even if it is just for loss leader products to stave off the buying migration to higher or lower price points.

Time your acceleration in economic cycles

Gauging how fast to invest in each particular cycle of the economy is a significant challenge. If your business invests too slowly, your competitors will win the race to the market. If your business invests too quickly, your business increases its risks and the chance of failure.

American Eagle outfitters is a midmarket retailer that has had strong business success. They made a business decision to open a high-end retail version of their store called Martin + Osa. These stores were targeted toward the high-end consumer between 25 and 40 years old. They built beautiful stores and were selling merchandise at premium prices but they had not strongly established that high-end brand in the marketplace when the economy contracted. The Gap, another retail store with a strong business success, decided to open a series of women's high-end stores. Shortly thereafter, the economy began contracting and they were forced to close those stores. One retailer mused that when Target store sales increase three months in a row that will be a sign that the recovery is underway.

Figure 5.2

Unbundle products/services in economic contractions, bundle in expansions

A good rule of thumb is to unbundle products and services in an economic contraction and bundle them in expansions and recoveries. The logic is that when the economy contracts, more consumers are placing the "lowest price" dimension of the value proposition as the high priority. As the economy expands, customers are more willing to pay a higher price for bundled services as the lowest price dimension migrates down their priority list. As economies contract, consumers migrate to higher price sensitivities.

Businesses have several choices to respond to this migration of price sensitivity. They can lower costs and cut into margins. An alternative is to look at services that are bundled into existing product offerings and determine which services are less important to customers relative to how much it costs the business to provide those services. This will enable the business to migrate to a lower cost platform for its customers' new lowest-priced priority while minimizing the effect on margin. One of the keys to success is to discover areas of cost-cutting that have the minimum impact on customer experience and revenue generation.

As the economy began to show signs of contraction, one major airline observed increased sensitivity to "lowest price" by a broad segment of their customers. They began scrutinizing their flights to determine the operational costs of each of their bundled services relative to the degree to which customers utilized those services. They found that several services e.g. checked bags, meals, alcoholic drinks, had low utilization rates by many segments of both their business and leisure travel markets. In terms of baggage, they found that only a small percentage of their business travelers checked baggage. They found that leisure travelers only checked bags roughly half the time. The handling, transporting, and tracking of baggage represent a significant operational cost to their airline and an excellent area to focus on. Their objective in doing this was to achieve a better position for addressing their customers' new sensitivity for lowest priced offerings in the market while still protecting their brand integrity as a high-quality airline. They segmented a new baggage policy by frequent flyer status, international/domestic travelers, and baggage weight. They also created a pricing structure that encouraged behavioral change in other passengers relative to how many belongings they brought on either a business or personal trip. Prior to this new baggage policy, passengers had a tremendous amount of leeway to carry with them a significant amount of personal belongings without any financial penalty. Now, with a financial penalty in place, consumers began to carry fewer personal belongings. It was also very helpful that the entire industry migrated in this direction, which created a new norm for baggage policies. While some of their customers would regard these charges as "nuisance" charges, most customers would accept them because of the simple fact that only a minority of travelers would actually be affected financially and most of the travelers could avoid any financial penalty by just being more frugal in what they brought on trips.

Understand the change in the money stream

In prosperous economies, businesses typically subcontract much more of their business activities. This money stream in these situations needs to be well understood so that quiet changes can be made in changing economic times.

One tools manufacturer would target subcontracting between 15% and 20% of their production to act as a production "rubber band" at a slight premium. They could quickly increase or decrease the subcontracting quantity to match marketplace economics. They have invested in their ability to change over their product manufacturing more quickly; their production runs during the latest downturn are half the size (from 100 down to 50) they were in a prosperous economy.

A strategy specific to boom periods

Don't overextend your business in good times

One major UK retailer made significant changes to consolidate the business back toward the areas where they had a high level of expertise while the economy was still strong. Their strategy was simple: To reorganize and consolidate toward our strengths. This enables them to be able to weather almost any economic downturn. The key was not to overextend beyond their capabilities. At one point during their business history, they had outlets across countries like the US and Australia particularly residing in hotels and airports. Such a diverse global business infrastructure "stretched" the business's capabilities to properly maintain their retail market on a global basis. Even though they had expanded globally, much of their new expansion was only generating marginal profits. Once the new CEO was on board, he made a decision to direct them "back to basics" where they can effectively drive and manage the cost base of their business. Once they consolidated their geographic and core competencies, they began to leverage information technology to drive not only general operational efficiency but also to tune this efficiency relative to the various economic cycles.

Building a barrier to entry

A business must understand how their product or service helps build a barrier to entry for the competitors of their potential client. Here are some dimensions of their barriers to entry.

* **Advertising.** Incumbent businesses can make it difficult for new competitors by spending heavily on advertising that new organizations would find more difficult to afford. This is known as the **market power theory of advertising.** Here, an established organization's use of advertising creates a consumer perceived difference in its brand relative to other brands to a degree that consumers see that its brand is noticeably different. Since the brand is seen as offering a slightly different product, products from existing or potential competitors cannot be perfectly substituted in place of the established businesses' brand.

This makes it more difficult for new competitors to gain consumer acceptance.

- **Cost advantages independent of scale.** Proprietary technology, intellectual property and the skills to implement it, ready access to raw materials, favorable geographic locations, learning curve cost advantages.

- **Customer loyalty.** Large incumbent businesses may have existing customer relationships that have high loyalty to established products. The presence of established strong brands within a market can be a barrier to entry in this case.

- **Distributor agreements.** Exclusive contracts with key distributors or retailers can make it difficult for other manufacturers to enter the market.

- **Economy of scale.** Large, experienced businesses can produce goods at lower costs than small, less experienced businesses. Cost advantages can many times be reversed by technology advancements. For example, the development of personal computers has allowed small companies to make use of database and web technologies which was once extremely expensive and only available to large, sophisticated businesses.

- **Globalization.** Entry of global players into local markets make entry of local players into the market more difficult.

- **Government regulations.** It may make entry more difficult or impossible. In the extreme case, a government may make competition against the law and establish a legal monopoly. Requirements for licenses and permits may raise the investment needed to enter a market, creating an effective economic barrier to entry.

- **Inelastic demand.** A strategy of selling at a lower price in order to penetrate markets. This does not work with price-insensitive consumers.

- **Intellectual property.** Potential entrant requires access to equally efficient production technology as the competitor monopolist in order to freely enter a market. Patents give an organization the legal right to stop other organizations producing a product for a given period of time, and so stop entry into a market. Patents are intended to encourage invention and technological innovation by offering this financial incentive. Similarly, trademarks and servicemarks may represent a kind of entry barrier for a particular product or service if the market is dominated by one or a few well-known brand names.

- **Investment.** That is especially in industries with economies of scale and/or large natural monopolies.
- **Network effect.** When a good or service has a value that depends on the number of existing customers, then competing players may have difficulties in entering a market where an established business has already captured the majority of the customer base.
- **Predatory pricing.** The practice of a dominant organization selling at a loss to make competition more difficult for new businesses that cannot suffer losses of the magnitude that a larger dominant business can sustain. It is illegal in most places; however, it is difficult to prove.
- **Restrictive practices,** such as air transport agreements, that make it difficult for new airlines to obtain landing slots at some airports or routes to new geographic areas.
- **Research and development.** Some products, such as microprocessors or communication processors, require a large upfront investment in technology which will deter potential entrants.
- **Supplier agreements.** Exclusive and restrictive agreements with key links in the supply chain can make it difficult for other manufacturers to enter an industry.
- **Sunk costs.** Sunk costs cannot be recovered if an organization decides to leave a market and not return. Sunk costs therefore increase the risk and deter entry.

- **Vertical integration.** An organization's coverage of more than one level of production, while pursuing practices which favor its own field operations at each level, is often cited as an entry barrier.*

Be cautious with switching costs

For switching costs, your business needs to understand how your product or service can help build in switching costs for your potential client's "clients".

There are several types of switching costs (Klemperer, 1987a): (a) transaction costs (e.g., changing your bank), (b) learning costs (e.g., changing cell phones), and (c) contractual costs (e.g., frequent-shopper programs). One of the most frequently used approaches that organizations used to build in costs of switching are reward programs (e.g., frequent shopper clubs, frequent flyer programs). These programs are not without significant cost and do not guarantee a positive ROI (Dowling & Uncles, 1997). Program effectiveness only occurs when consumers actually change their habits and behave in a more loyal manner as a direct result of the program (O'Brien & Jones, 1995). Other approaches for creating switching costs include restricting the functionality of software, or segmenting levels of service. The question still remains whether any program which creates artificial switching costs actually creates sustainable added value to the business.

Switching costs is having a direct impact on customer retention and also the competitive dynamics of a market. If a customer has a cost to switch products P and is currently buying from organization A, assuming the products are similar, a second organization B has to offer a price PB < PA

---

*Source: Wikipedia.

in order to prompt the customer to change products. In this case, switching costs can potentially change demand inelastic and therefore reduce competition among businesses in the market (e.g., Klemperer, 1987a, b). In this highly informated marketplace, businesses can quite closely calculate a consumer's switching cost with advanced analytics, they can surgically target consumers with precise offers and pricing, making switching much more difficult. Locking in consumers in such a way will increase competition in the marketplace as businesses gain market share (Klemperer, 1987a). This could create potential future negative impacts such as decreasing consumers reference pricing and cost of switching. If consumers behave logically, they will recognize the implications of locking themselves into one product supplier, and demand lower prices at the beginning of the relationship. This will likely increase price competition in the initial market. These switching costs are typically dynamic and can be greatly influenced by the experience of the product or service. Switching costs can also be highly dynamic on the web where switching costs are typically lower end highly dynamic and price-sensitive. The Web as a delivery channel is unique in this area. The ease of comparison shopping and moving from supplier to supplier is radically different than in the off-line world, e.g. visiting stores (Alba *et al.*, 1997, Bakos, 1991, 1997). Nevertheless, loyalty on the Internet has been found to be higher than in the offline world (Brynjolfsson & Smith, 2000) and it has also been argued that consumers present lock-in effects on the Web and do not search as much as expected (Johnson *et al.*, 2004, Zauberman, 2003). For example, Johnson *et al.* (2004) using Mediametrix data have modeled visits behavior of a group of customers in the music category. It was found that consumers search far less than expected, presenting evidence that lock-in effects exist even on the web. Zauberman (2003) using an experiment that studied consumer behavior in a travel agency, also presents evidence of "lock-in" effects and what he defines as "consumer's myopia": consumers could not effectively anticipate future switching costs. Therefore, even though logic suggests that the characteristics of the Web as a purchasing channel would reduce consumers' switching costs, this has not been empirically proven.*

References

Alba, J., Lynch, J., Weitz, B., Janiszewski, C. & others (1997) Interactive home shopping: Consumer, retailer, and manufacturer incentives to participate in electronic marketplaces, *Journal of Marketing*, **61**(3), 38–53.

Bakos, J.Y. (1991) A strategic analysis of electronic marketplaces, *Mis Quarterly*, **15**(3), 295–310.

Bakos, J.Y. (1997) Reducing buyer search costs: Implications for electronic marketplaces, *Management Science*, **43**(12), 1676–1692.

Brynjolfsson, E. & Smith, M.D. (2000) Frictionless commerce? A comparison of internet and conventional retailers. *Management Science*, **46**(4), 563–585.

Dowling, G.R. & Uncles, M. (1997) Do customer loyalty programs really work? *Sloan Management Review*, **38**(4), 71–82.

Johnson, E.J., Moe, W.W., Fader P.S., Bellman S. & Lohse, G.L. (2004) On the depth and dynamics of online search behaviour, *Management Science*, **50**(3), 299–308.

Klemperer, P. (1987a) The competitiveness of markets with switching costs, *Rand Journal of Economics*, **18**(1), 138–150.

Klemperer, P. (1987b) Markets with consumer switching costs, *Quarterly Journal of Economics*, **102**(2), 375–394.

O'Brien, L. & Jones, C. (1995) Do rewards really create loyalty? *Harvard Business Review*, **73**(3), 75–82.

Zauberman, G. (2003) The intertemporal dynamics of consumer lock-in, *Journal of Consumer Research*, **30**(3), 405–419.

*Source: The essence of knowledge – NOW

B2B Approaches for Different Economic Cycles

6

There is a wide range of business approaches and strategies to address how economic cycles change the way businesses buy. These strategies range from a simple focus on reducing your customer's costs to complete business transformation. Below are several examples that illustrate a range of business approaches in different economic cycles. Particularly for nonboom economies, building the B2B business case is a critical skill for any business. This chapter also provides a full range of business case approaches and examples that will provide powerful tools for a business to help quantify their value proposition.

Create pay-for-performance market initiatives

At one tool manufacturer, their clients will frequently ask them to make a tool to test against their competitors. Being sure to establish the success criteria beforehand so that it constitutes a strong agreement or contract between the two parties is a necessity. In their case, such success criteria would be tool life, surface finish, and accuracy of the bore. Typically, in competitor environments, the criteria of success will constitute a significant improvement over their current suppliers' performance.

Pay-for-performance initiatives are showing a significant increase in the midst of a contracting economy and in a recession. The popularity of pay-for-performance buying subsides during recovering economies and they are least practiced in prospering economies. The increase in businesses using performance buying is roughly 15%–25% in contracted economies. This makes sense because, during prosperous economies, the focus is on getting a product out the door to realize the margins on your sales ... as business and financial capital constricts, the shift toward cost and margin control is much more important.

A contracted economy has too much capacity, too many people chasing fewer sales opportunities. Therefore pay-for-performance is a guaranteed way to minimize or eliminate risks while at the same time investing in production costs that have guaranteed cost efficiency.

Make it embarrassing NOT to buy from your business

One manufacturer in tough times has focused on selling cost savings rather than other classic sales approaches. When their sales people are selling into an "old boy network", the CEO says that they make it "embarrassing" if they don't choose them because of their significant cost savings. One example he gave was their efforts to sell into a large North American automotive manufacturer. He said that these particular buyers had been buying their competitor's tools for many years and they were not going to change their purchasing unless there was some radical value difference in their particular products. In their current production environment, they could manufacturer 7000 engine blocks without requiring a tool change. The sales team asked the ultimate question – what level of performance would it take to buy from us? The large manufacturer told them that it would take a manufacturing run of 50,000 engine blocks without a tool change to get their business. With their new tools, they were able to boost that production run to 200,000 engine blocks without a tool change. It would have been an embarrassment for them not to buy their tools.

Create good products in good times and great products in tough times

A US tool manufacturer strategy wants to make products that have a good value proposition in prosperous economies and a great value proposition in tougher economies. The CEO commented that this strategy "saved their bacon" when the economy contracted. Their strategy was to be the easiest business to do business with. For this organization, that meant creating products that were tailored to a diversity of customer applications, not biased toward how much it would cost to produce this particular product. They targeted 60% of their business to specialize in tools that had multiple applications and could reduce their clients' manufacturing costs significantly relative to more generic one-use products.

In creating their products, they would look at their customer's business, figure out what was the most cost-effective way for them to run their business, and then create the tools that would enable that for not only one type of machine but multiple machines. In prosperous times, this approach had obvious benefits but when the economy contracted, the advantages of this type of approach had a far bigger economic impact and therefore helped sustain revenue growth not only for their client but for themselves.

To take an example: one of their larger clients was in the design stages to produce a very advanced V6 engine. They took the time to examine the manufacturing operations and learned that their current production for the cylinder head and the block would require 25 different types of retoolings to execute the machining operations. They took the time to understand their tooling operation and engineered their products to reduce the 25 tools down to five tools. Not only is this more efficient, but it reduces their inventory costs, their SKU management issues, and simplifies ordering.

Address the social spending stigma

JetBlue Airlines is an innovative company and took a unique approach to the corporate jet debacles. JetBlue took out a full-page ad in the *LA Times* addressing the uproar against executives using private corporate jets. Their campaign's message basically was "If you still want to fly with all the luxury amenities that you are used to having in your corporate jets, e.g. private video monitors, full leather seats, cocktails, and you don't want to incur the wrath of negative public opinion about using your corporate jets, come fly with us. We can have all the luxury amenities that you're use to when flying and do it without guilt … i.e. 'we've got you covered.'"

Business transformation

Economic cycles can be the optimum time for businesses to transform themselves. This transformation can either come from opportunity or necessity. The following examples reveal how tough economic times prompted several businesses to look beyond a myopic view of their market and leverage new opportunities. Marketing myopia is a term used in marketing as well as the title of an important marketing paper written by Theodore Levitt. This paper was first published in 1960 in the *Harvard Business Review*, a journal of which he was an editor.

Some commentators have suggested that its publication marked the beginning of the modern marketing movement. Its theme is that the vision of most organizations is too constricted by a narrow understanding of what business they are in. It exhorted CEOs to re-examine their corporate vision; and redefine their markets in terms of wider perspectives. It was successful in its impact because it was, as with all of Levitt's work, essentially practical and pragmatic. Organizations found that they had been missing opportunities that were plain to see once they adopted the wider view. The paper was influential. The oil companies (which represented one of his main examples in the paper) redefined their business as energy rather than just petroleum, although Royal Dutch Shell, which embarked upon an investment program in nuclear power, subsequently regretted this course of action.

One reason that short sightedness is so common is that people feel that they cannot accurately predict the future. While this is a legitimate concern, it is also possible to use a whole range of business prediction techniques currently available to estimate future circumstances as well as possible.

There is a greater scope for opportunities as the industry changes. It trains managers to look beyond their current business activities and think "outside the box". George Steiner (1979) claims that if a buggy whip manufacturer in 1910 defined its business as the "transportation starter business", they might have been able to make the creative leap necessary to move into the automobile business when technological change demanded it.

People who focus on marketing strategy, various predictive techniques, and the customer's lifetime value can rise above myopia to a certain extent. This can entail the use of long-term profit objectives (sometimes at the risk of sacrificing short-term objectives). It can also result in marketers being caught unawares with quick economic cycle changes.

Smart organizations realize this. They also realize that even in good times, consumers' attention is a scarce commodity. In bad times, that attention remains scarce but the focus and the expectations increase expediently.

Complicating things further, the not so smart marketers just turn up the volume on their same old messaging. As a result, marketplace noise increases, the relative abundance of attention becomes scarcer, and consumers become increasingly numb.

The smart marketers shift focus from quantity to quality – adapting to how they know consumers are feeling and viewing the world.*

Understand what your business really does

One professional web services company with a managed services model was finding it difficult to compete when orders declined by 40% in a major recession. Chargeable rates were down 10 to 15%. Clients were squeezing margins across the board. They were in the business of providing manpower to help with content creation. The clients would no longer be allowed to spend money on "manpower" so the funding dried up for the web services company. This web services company had to change how they offered their services in conjunction with where the money could flow to clients. Instead of charging for manpower, they charged

*Source: Wikipedia.

for pieces of created content. The clients could then find this type of service. This web services company also found that instead of targeting small pieces of business, they could actually address large gaps in their clients' web content areas because whole departments were being cut out. So instead of their market becoming smaller, it actually became larger once they stepped back and looked at the entire business model.

A large homebuilder in the US found that their market almost completely dried up when the real estate market severely contracted. It was a desperate time for this builder. They had to creatively figure out a way to create new business in an extremely contracted economy. They asked themselves "What do we really do?" "We build houses" was the myopic answer. The broader answer was "We build things". With this revelation, they discovered that there was a market for building prefabricated walls which were much quicker and less expensive to supply to the marketplace than having builders create house walls on location. This change in strategy saved their business and gave them the financial strength they needed to ride out the contracted real estate market.

A manufacturer who assembled automobile mirrors was dramatically hit by the downturn in the automotive industry. What business were they really in? They assembled automobile side mirrors. That was the myopic answer. The broader answer was that they assembled subassemblies. Having stepped back from their market, they started marketing themselves as an assembly company. They soon won a major contract to assemble food blenders which gave them a solid revenue stream to survive the contraction of the economy.

Mergers and acquisitions

As businesses enter into economies or markets that are contracting or are in recession, the valuations of the businesses are likely going to be relatively low. This is an excellent time to look for compatible businesses to either buy with cash or in stock exchange. One manufacturer is currently visiting all of their competitors to assess what the value of their current business is either from a customer list perspective, equipment, or production capability. The CEO comments, "I am visiting all of our competitors with the idea of acquisition." He adds, "There will be a lot of businesses that aren't going to weather the economic downturns."

Once businesses have been identified for potential acquisition targets, acquisitions need to be executed prior to an economic upturn to leverage the best price for the acquisition. Ideally, it is also when credit will start freeing up a bit to address any financing as well. Terms of the acquisition can range from a cash purchase to exchange of stock. The CEO commented that one of the targeted companies wanted to be purchased and because of their current size and debt load, the only reasonable strategy was to simply take over the company and give the taken-over company company stock so that they would benefit on the backend.

One of the critical dynamics of businesses moving through economic transitions is the opportunity to transform themselves. In many cases, the most challenging economic times provide the most opportunity for innovation. The biggest challenge is moving beyond "marketing myopia".

Building the B2B business case

Times are tough. Businesses are scared. Money is tight. Budgets are cut. Hurdle rates are raised. Sound familiar? No matter what you're selling, the importance of the business case has just reached a whole new level of importance. Without a compelling business case for your product or service, your customers and prospects will not buy from you.

In hard times, businesses consciously shut certain money flows off and allow other money flows to continue but at reduced rates. The objective is to:

(a) assess where and how money is still flowing (or not flowing) for your prospective client;
(b) understand and then position your value proposition toward that money flow;
(c) quantify the impact your value proposition will have on that area.

It is relatively easy to interview insiders within your prospective customer to understand where the money sensitivities lie. While it is not necessary or practical to engage the CFO, this is helpful if they are amenable to a meeting. Once you have built a schematic of how the money is now flowing, you must reassess your value proposition relative to that new flow and how your products or services impact that flow.

Build your business case models for different economies and transitions

Businesses typically build business cases for their products and services for the current economy with no explicit iterations for significant contraction or expansion of the economy. This would be akin to building an automobile without windshield wipers. Businesses need to proactively build several different models of their business case to buy based on several different levels of economic activity.

One particular tool manufacturer has a tool cost of valuation spreadsheet with specific highlighted components for prosperous economies and specific elements for contracted economies. For prospering economies, potential customers can enter variables that will project how much margin per machine, e.g. $6,500 additional margins generated by machine A per month if they use this manufacturer's cutting tools. If the economy has contracted, there are specific elements that are more focused on reduction of production costs and efficiency of tool use, e.g. tool changeover, extra measurements, deburring (secondary "cost of quality" operational costs to manufacturing). Most of his businesses start to think about purchasing their tools in terms of out-of-pocket and indirect costs. With their spreadsheet, the client can plug in the margin of their manufactured product using their tools which produces a "what if" scenario, e.g. if you can produce X more additional units per month on machine Y, then your company will generate an additional Z margin using our tools on that particular machine.

Human aspects of the business case

Let's begin by understanding the fundamentals of the business case. The common fallacy is that business cases are about rational and rigorous numbers. Not true. The core of a business case is how key influencers and decision-makers "feel" about the numbers, i.e. do they believe them/view. A common mistake is for people to build spreadsheets in their office and then populate them with numbers independent of any process or buy-in from the prospective client.

The best business cases are not pre-manufactured in a cubicle and then "thrown over the wall". Each one must be customized to the business. Not only customized to the business, but the numbers contained in the business case must be emotionally tied to someone important who not only believes them but has the power to act on them. The perfect business case is one which, when finally presented to the decision-makers, the "numbers" have already been emotionally "bought into".

The most effective business cases are those that are built with people who are perceived as the nonbiased experts within the business. The process of actually creating the "numbers" that will populate the business case should involve these people from the beginning of the process. In essence, you are building their human bias into the numbers as well as their support of the numbers. In doing this, when the formal business case is presented, it will have already been agreed to and sanctioned by the people who carry the most weight in terms of their internal trust factor or unbiased nature as subject matter experts.

When a vendor presents "their" numbers, the trust factor is typically around 20% based on extrapolations of the Edelman Trust Index. When the number is tied to an internally trusted, unbiased individual, the trust factor ranges anywhere from 60 to 90% depending on the strengths of the following two factors:

1. Perception of being unbiased
2. Perception of degree of expertise.

These internally trusted subject matter experts (SMEs) should be the ones that the funding person/s regards as the de facto expert with no particular bias or vested interest in the decision to buy or not to buy. An effective way to achieve this is to create a business case "committee". This committee not only includes the decision-makers but also the trusted, independent SMEs. The very process of them being a part of the committee is your chance to subtly sell them and build their biases into the "numbers". As the business case committee works to prepare the business case, you are transparently and subtly selling them as well as understanding their beliefs and biases toward the potential impact of your product or solution on their business.

Creativity is the key – traditional versus nontraditional business case approaches

Once the committee is established, and you understand how money flows in this economic environment, you must choose which approach will most effectively portray the potential impact of your product or service on your prospective client.

In tough economic times, creativity is the key. It is important to understand the full range of both traditional and nontraditional business case approaches. There are multiple approaches to business cases. Some are traditional, such as revenue generation, mitigating revenue risk, cost displacement, and cost avoidance. Typically these traditional measures are expressed in financial metrics and are targeted toward current results.

There are also lots of nontraditional measures for business cases that are more operational in nature and whose focus is on future results. Examples of these approaches are customer satisfaction (e.g. net promoter/detractor scores), Work Value, cost and quality, option value, technical importance (infrastructure investing), competitive advantage, and value of customers over time (customer lifetime revenue).

Figure 6.1 depicts these approaches.

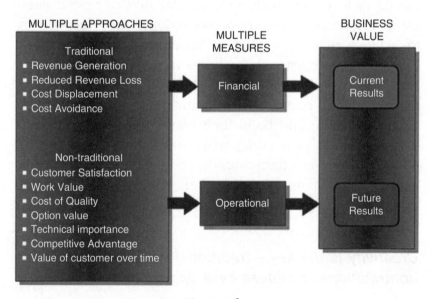

Figure 6.1

The Internet/Web extends these nontraditional approaches to measurements distinctly directed at online environments. These measures are constantly evolving and maturing with new advanced forms of web analytics, e.g. Sales, Leads, Conversions, Subscribers, Usability metrics, Returning visitors, Pageviews per visit, Time on page, Time on site, Bounce rate, Form/shopping cart abandonment rate, Next pages, Links clicked (heat maps), Eyetracking, Internal searches, SEO metrics, Number of backlinks, Quality of backlinks, Google cache date, Google bot (robot) visit frequency, Last time Google bot visited, Pages indexed, PageRank "pass rate", Alexa Rank, Compete Rank, Social Media metrics, Bookmarks on delicious, Bookmarks elsewhere, Social news submissions, Tweets (Twitter mentions), Niche social site sites votes, Number of "thumbs up" on StumbleUpon, StumbleUpon reviews feedback, Technorati Blog mentions, Google BlogSearch Links.

Building the right business case to buy in tough times

In tough economic times, the importance of the measures shifts depending on the stage of the economy. In general, the importance of revenue generation gives way to revenue protection. There also is a movement from revenue-related business metrics to cost displacement and avoidance.

Big impact versus fast impact

In a troubled economy, the emphasis is also directed toward fast and tactical versus big and strategic gains. While this is a movement within the dimensions of traditional approaches, there also is a predominant focus on this category relative to nontraditional measures. This migration happens even

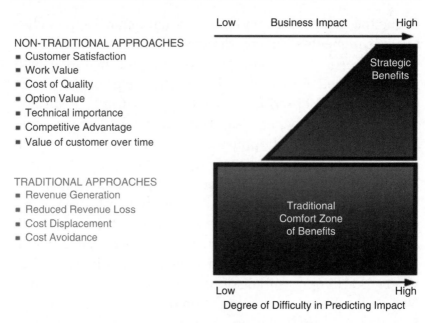

Figure 6.2

though the impact of nontraditional measures can eclipse the impact of traditional measures in the long term.

One might think that using the nontraditional approaches would be a waste of effort in a down economy. This is not the case. Powerful approaches such as Work Value and cost of quality can do much to fundamentally change the cost structures a business wrestles with in troubled times.

When building a business case, businesses must first understand how their product impacts their prospective customers' financial and operational success factors.

This, in and of itself, is an important step but worthless by itself. Unless your customer is a monopoly, they will always have choices and therefore you will need to understand how your business impacts your prospective customers' business relative to your competition's impact.

Strategic, nontraditional approaches

While the nature of most strategic nontraditional approaches is mid- to long-term in payback time frames, they can easily be executed to deliver short-term cost reduction and avoidance impact.

Work Value

Work Value is a strategic approach to optimizing the time associates spend at the task commensurate with their level of compensation. This approach is typically used to increase the time a person spends adding value at the level at which they were hired to add value. This approach can be used to create both long-term and short-term cost efficiencies. The objective is to understand how your product or service can increase the time your customers and employees expend on task at an appropriate work level.

For example, how does your product or service allow the director of marketing to spend more time on marketing strategy than on administrative type functions? In the Work Value approach, not only do you get cost efficiencies by allowing a high powered director to spend more time doing higher skilled work rather than performing lower skilled work which could be done by a significantly less compensated employee. The other dimension of this is that the business will ultimately end up developing better marketing programs.

To take an example: An automotive tools manufacturer has a value proposition that helps shift manufacturer workers to higher value positions. There are tools to reduce manufacturing preparation and checking positions, e.g. tool setting, or quality measurement, so those people can be reallocated to higher value positions, e.g. machine operators, machine programmers. This is part of their value proposition of creating a consistently high-quality product. This Work Value approach is in parallel to a cost of quality advantage as well.

Cost of quality

Cost of quality is another typically strategic business case approach, which is a dimension of Total Quality Management (TQM). TQM is a business management strategy focused on embedding awareness of quality in organizational processes. The "cost" of quality is not the cost of creating a quality product or service but the cost of *not* creating a quality product or service. This "cost" can be used to illustrate the business impact of your product or service if your product or service reduces costs associated with poor quality.

When determining how your product or service could impact your potential customers' attributes of quality in their processes, you can analyze any scope of activities that can be affected by your product. For example, if your product is designed to improve the efficiency and effectiveness of both a sales and marketing organization, Figure 6.3 illustrates how you would view your product's or service's impact from a cost of quality perspective.

There are two dimensions of cost and quality that must be examined.

Figure 6.3

Refering to Figure 6.3, aligning your product or service to their impact on cost of quality dimensions will follow this list of cost of quality areas:

- Essential first-time work – work activities required for Sales and Marketing in an ideal environment.
- Cost of quality work.
- Prevention – investment to prevent nonconformance with customer requirements.
- Appraisal – cost to measure conformance to customer requirements.
- Rework/Failure – cost of failing to meet customer requirements.
  - Internal rework/failure – activities that occur before product or service is delivered to external customer;
  - External rework/failure – activities that occur after product or service is delivered to external customer.

COQ assumptions and measurements

- Three fundamental assumptions:
  - Failures are caused
  - Prevention is cheaper
  - Performance can be measured
- Typical measures include:
  - Percentage of revenue
  - Percentage of profit
  - Percentage of cost of goods sold
  - Percentage of operating budget.

COQ industry metrics

Industries
- 30% of sales (Crosby projections)
- 25% of sales (Juran projections)
- 35–70% in service industries (Juran projections)

Corporations

* Corning Glass – 25–30% of revenue
* IBM – 26% of revenue.

Cost of Quality Matrix (%)

In order to understand what impact your product or service has on the business you are trying to sell you must map the impact of your product against these five dimensions:

Activity

% of time spent
Essential, first-time activity
Prevention activity
Appraisal activity
Failure activity

In the illustration below, a business is showing how their customer relationship management solution can shift out their potential customers' dimensions of cost and quality.

Essential, first-time work

In this example, the proposed solution would increase the amount of time the business they are attempting to sell their solution to could spend on their fundamental activity of:

1. Targeting new customers
2. Contacting those target customers
3. Acquiring those customers.

The time and resources saved from their solution enables the business to now initiate new marketing activities. Previously, there was no bandwidth to extend their marketing campaigns because of cost of quality issues, e.g. inefficiency of targeting, low effectiveness of contacting a customer, low uptake from an ineffective offer.

Prevention

In the prevention category, your proposed solution could be positioned to show how you help the business save time and money by not contacting customers or prospects with low propensities to buy.

Appraisal

In the appraisal category, your solution can be positioned to show how it increases the effectiveness of customers who have a high propensity to purchase. Also in the appraisal category, your solution could be positioned to show how it helps target more profitable customers

Rework/failure

In the rework/failure category, your solution can be positioned to illustrate how your prospective customer can (by choosing the right customer) reduce multiple contacts and thus have less investing in prospective customers who have a low propensity to buy – essentially shifting time and money to selling and marketing high probability and profitable customers.

Looking at the potential impact on an income statement, you can see where your solution could have potential impact on the bottom line. For example, under cost of sales quality costs, your solution may impact such things as production testing, scrap/rework/re-inspection, obsolescence/damage, and returned goods.

In terms of the potential bottom-line impact on selling and administrative quality costs, your solution may have the potential for impacting such things as premium freight

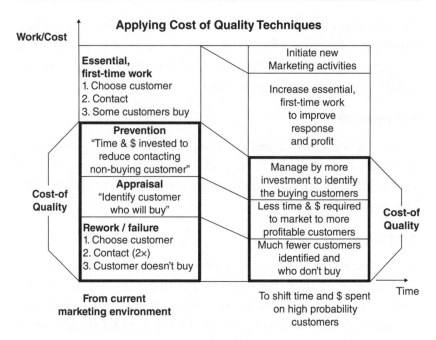

Figure 6.4

charges, warehousing costs, marketing research, and sales force productivity.

In terms of your solution's potential impact on research and development quality costs, it is important to explore how your new solution may impact the product research and development and the time to market.

In terms of your solution's potential impact on interest expense quality costs, it is important to explore such items as time and rate flexibility and accuracy, management information, funds management, and reaction to prime rate.

In terms of noninterest expense quality costs, your product or service may impact such things as recovery costs, training cost, compliance costs, systems overhead, and marketing (new product development and time-to-market).

Option value is another traditional approach that is worth exploring in terms of your solution's impact on the prospective customer.

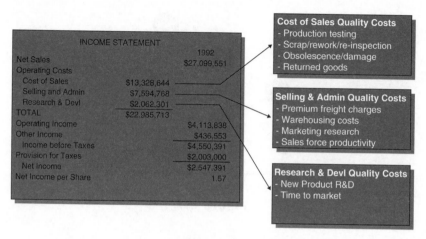

Figure 6.5

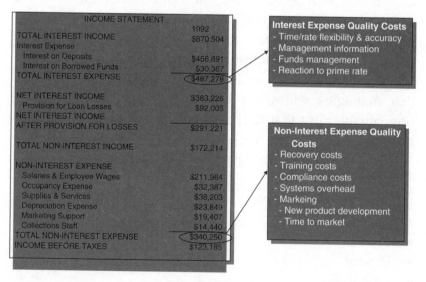

Figure 6.6

Source: David J. Sharp.

Whether your business is selling technology or non technologically oriented services, projects are typically internally justified on the basis of some form of net-present-value (NPV) criterion. Using NPV has limited effectiveness for

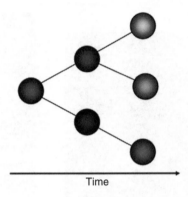

Time

Figure 6.7

investment appraisal. The "present value" of an investment's cash flows excludes the valuable options embedded within the investment (your product or service). These options give your potential customer the ability to take advantage of certain business opportunities later.

The threat to competitiveness lies not in the possibility that managers will select investments that turn out to be unprofitable, but that they will fail to undertake very risky, but strategically vital, ones.

Figure 6.8 shows the option value decision tree:

Options can be weighted by:

- Cost
- Benefit
- Probability
- Other factors.

In each node of the decision tree moving forward, the option that it creates or provides can be weighted by costs and benefits with the probability of occurrence. Besides costs and benefits, almost any investment determinant can be weighed in this option schema.

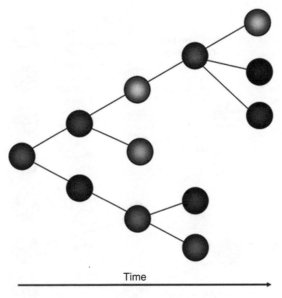

Time

Figure 6.8

As Figure 6.9 shows, not only is the business weighing its decisions but also weighing the probability of competitors' responses as well as customer responses in multiple scenarios.

For example: An automotive tool manufacturer produces a milling cutter that has the flexibility for being used for several different operations. The teeth on the cutting body can be changed out to give it many new manufacturing job applications. This capability is a strong competitive advantage because their competitors' cutting bodies are designed for only one manufacturing operation and if the product is at the end of its life cycle, the manufacturer essentially throws away $300–$3000 in cutting tools because of their narrow application design.

Figure 6.10 illustrates an option schema populated with cash flows, present value without abandonment, and present value with abandonment. Starting with the organization's

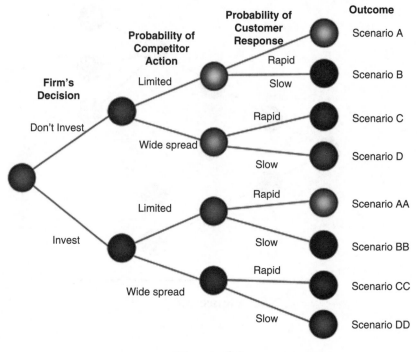

Figure 6.9

investment (in millions); filtered with a probability of 50% of a particular competitor's response; filtered again by the probability of a particular customer's response; filtered again with an additional probability and an outcome with the present value of future cash flows in multiple scenarios.

The scenario runs along a three-year timeframe assuming that year 1 requires basic research, year 2 requires clinical testing, and year 3 is the development phase.

Competitor advantage

Competitive advantage is an approach to building a business case for investment.

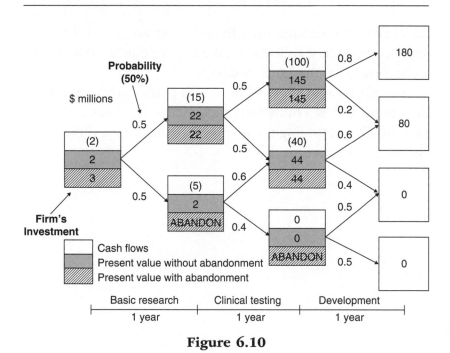

Figure 6.10

To understand this approach, the first questions which need to be asked for your product or solution relative to its impact on your customer or prospect are:

- Can your product or service build barriers to entry in your market?
- Can your product or service change the basis of competition?
- Can your product or service change the balance of power in supplier relationships?
- Can your product or service generate new products?*

When you are considering the value of your product, the competitive advantage approach suggests that your product or service will give your potential client not only competitive

*Source: McFarlan.

advantage but a differential between advantage and necessity, i.e. the time it is likely to take a competitive opportunity to become a competitive necessity.

The other value dimension of competitor advantage is to determine if this competitive advantage is sustainable, i.e. perpetually continuing the competitive advantage differential versus competitive necessity.

7 Mastering Information across Economic Cycles

At any time the quality of a business's information is an essential element to any success. More critical though is a business's core information competency. The more competent a business is at using its information at critical decision points, the more flexible the business can be. This is particularly true during periods of changing economies. Detailed information essentially allows you to fine-tune your business to any economic cycle.

For example: one UK large book and stationery retailer developed the information competency to efficiently manage the process of recalling books back to publishers after a predetermined period of time.

When sales of the books started dropping off, the publisher agreed to take the books back. This was an initiative to remove stock out of the business thereby reducing carrying costs. Previously, each individual buying area would have to separately determine what time the books should be returned to the publishers at a publisher's level of sales. New technology allowed the company to look at the individual store levels in terms of what books were selling or not selling. They could then instruct the individual stores as to what books to return, and when, to the publisher.

This capability took millions of pounds of stock out of the business that they previously would have had to fund. Not only did this increase efficiency and reduce costs of carrying book stock, they were also able to take one full time equivalent (FTE) out of each buying area and replace it with one central person managing this activity. It also enabled them to tailor how they managed these stock returns to individual publishers.

They have also reduced the number of store staff that serve customers. They have done this by introducing much more flexible work hours. Using the sales data, they profile the store transactions by time of day and then link this data up with staffing budgets relative to the busy and slow store hours during the day. They then negotiate their employment contracts with their staff to align with the working hours when customers need them most rather than the typical 9-to-5 work day.

These technology-enabled efficiencies allowed an overall back to basics refocus on what they did best: be a seller of books, stationery, newspapers, and magazines. The retrenchment back to these areas away from such areas as running hotel gift shops was all-critical in managing any business cycle.

They also realized that one of their core competencies is serving the traveling customer. As such, they have expanded their presence in airports, railway stations, and motorway service stations. These capabilities not only made them much "leaner" as a business but added to your business's flexibility when economies do expand and contract.

Their preparation for contracting economies did not happen overnight. They estimate that their initial exploration as to what changes to make in how they could run their business in the leanest and most flexible way began a transformation that occurred over a three to five-year period. Prior to making this transformation, they had been deemed by financial analysts as a business in decline. They were seen to have no clear strategy for how they would move forward in a way that would provide the expected year-on-year profits.

An important aspect of efficiency and flexibility is automating the decision-making process as much as possible. Previously, this retailer would generate a report to the different stores. The stores would then make a decision as to what type of merchandise they would carry and then enter that information into the system. Now, the system generates a suggestion of which merchandise to carry. If the store agrees with the computer's recommendation, the order is executed and automatically linked back to the operational system. These structured building blocks of operational efficiency and flexibility have proven an advantage across economic cycles. In contrast, for other retailers in their marketplace, economic contractions have been merciless.

Other retailers such as Woolworth's did not have these efficiency and flexibility "building blocks" to navigate economic expansions and contractions effectively. In addition, Woolworth's performance in good economic times still witnessed them accumulating a massive debt of £385 million. The absence of these building blocks relegated Woolworth's to survival (not prosperity) in good times and death when the economy contracted. All of Woolworths' 807 stores were forced to shut down in the beginning of 2009 as 27,000 jobs were eliminated signaling the closure of a retail chain that had been a fixture on Britain's High Streets for almost 100 years.

The examples above show the extremes that can occur along the continuum of information as a core business competency. However, competency is no longer enough, mastery is needed – especially during a downturn economic cycle.

On the road to information mastery

Organizations reported that the rewards on the road to mastery far exceeded most investments in more traditional functional initiatives and infrastructure. The reported bottom-line impacts could be categorized into two basic areas:

1. The value created from making better decisions
2. The value created from making better decisions faster.

The value created from making better decisions was initially perceived as being the primary area of value. The speed impacts of improved information competency were frequently overlooked.

Closer analysis revealed that higher levels of information competency significantly increased the speed of a organization's proactive and reactive market actions. Analysis showed that the speed aspects of information competency accounted for roughly half of the entire benefit. The speed at which organizations are able to react to change and respond to the market as they developed their level of competency was clearly devastating to lesser-developed organizations. The impact of speed created two areas of value:

1. Proactive speed
2. Reactive speed.

Proactive speed manifested itself in the ability to identify a market opportunity, enter it, and take a market segment before the competitors understood what had happened.

Reactive speed manifested itself when a business could respond to a competitor's attack in predetermined ways almost instantaneously.

Although their reactive speed increased, as they moved along the continuum of information competency, the need

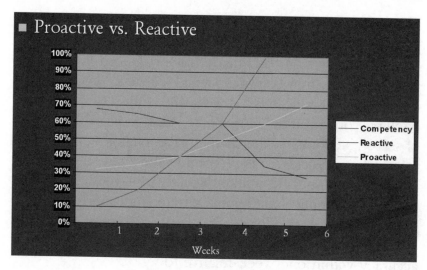

Figure 7.1

for reactive speed became less both for customers and competitors.

Before organizations began to travel down the road to mastery, they would experience a tremendous lag in their ability to react to market opportunities because of an inability to gather, analyze, and apply the required information. For example, one of the largest US investment brokers competed in a highly aggressive marketplace. In this example, they were anticipating changes in their market. Management felt that "… the market is going to recuperate; certain product segments would do well; and we know certain customers would probably buy …"

Having this market insight produced little benefit because once the market was targeted, it took two to four months to implement a marketing program because of their lack of ability to quickly apply the required market, customer, and operational information. Their Senior Vice President explained that it took: "… three months until we get our direct mail piece and marketing out". By the time they complete all of their information gathering, analysis, and implementation, the campaign is no longer appropriate because market conditions have changed.

After organizations had made more balanced investments in their information competency, their reaction times began to improve significantly. Another leading US investment banking organization comments that now they could observe conditions in the marketplace, change rapidly, and move very quickly. They commented that they could develop very specific marketing lists in several days relative to economic conditions as an indicator of likely behavior.

They could now answer questions with great speed and accuracy within one week relative to:

- Who is likely to respond to this promotion?
- Which are my most valuable prospects?
- Which of my customers are most vulnerable to competitive offers?

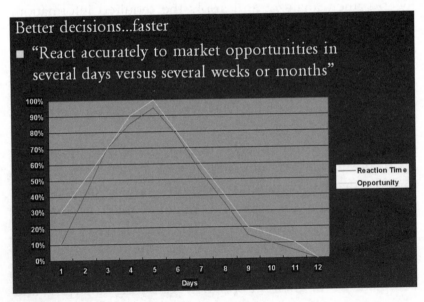

Figure 7.2

At a true information mastery level, 90% of the organization's resources are dedicated to proactive initiatives based on predictive capabilities. Their resources are centered on capturing business opportunities relative to consumer behavior, and then correlating that with economic conditions at the time. This is done with an advanced capability to:

- **Discover relationships.** Many buying behaviors may not be immediately discernible and can significantly improve targeting.
- **Provide correct weights in statistical models.** Income, geography, and previous responsiveness have determined how much revenue can be generated by each customer.
- **Simplify complexities of the business environment by advanced mathematics.** Marketing to a segment of "one" is simplified by scoring each customer, i.e. using more information more accurately.

Before the organizations started their journey on the road to mastery, they agreed that their reaction times to competitive attacks were either too slow, too uninformed, or both. In an economic cycle with any significant movement, either up or downward, this delay in reaction time can sound a company's death knell.

A leading US investment brokerage firm recounted a situation where their arch rival attacked one of their most profitable segments very late in the workweek hoping to get the jump on their best customers. After the organization realized what was occurring, they attempted to assess what the implications were for themselves as well as their customers. It took them two months to understand the financial implications of that attack. At this point, there were no formulated plans to counterattack, just an understanding of the financial implications. It took them another month to implement a counterattack, which they acknowledged was too little, too late.

The chart below (Figure 7.3) depicts the carnage.

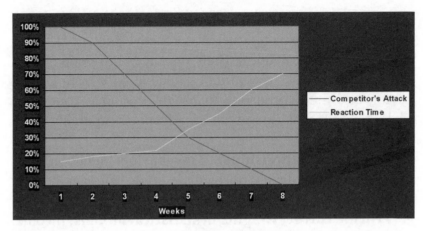

Figure 7.3

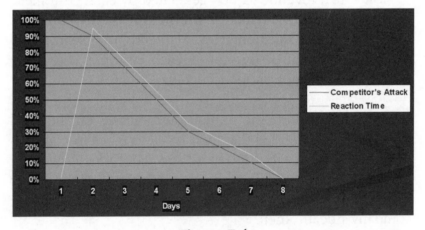

Figure 7.4

As organizations develop more information competency, they develop more speed. A major US investment banking organization recounted that their ability to currently react to a competitor's attack was almost instantaneous, accurate, and financially sound. This organization had the sophistication to pre-model almost all likely scenarios that a competitor would employ. When the competitors actually deployed one of these scenarios, they could assemble an accurate and sound response within two business days. Again, the master predicts and therefore can be proactive. This US investment banker's resources are focused not only on pre-emptive strikes but also on creating real value for customers in order to protect their best customers.

Information mastery and sales

A major US long distance telecommunications organization had a significant challenge of applying information to sales opportunities in a timely fashion. Under the old information environment, when the information regarding new sales leads would finally be put into action, the business environment had changed and the leads were irrelevant.

Before this organization started on the road to mastery, it would take them an average of six weeks to respond to a sales lead with a volume of 90 million records per year. This was at a cost of $0.35 per lead. As this telecommunications organization developed its information competency, it could respond to a lead in two hours with a volume of 150 million records per year. The cost of these leads dropped to $0.06 per lead. They further dropped to $0.04 per lead.

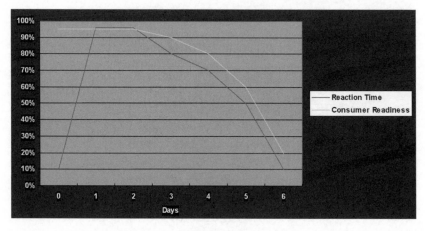

Figure 7.5

As this organization begins to approach information mastery, predicted response to lead will occur within the hour, with greater sales lead volumes. The cost of these leads is predicted to drop to $0.02 per lead.

Information mastery and profitability

As organizations progressed to higher levels of information competency, the relative awareness of profitability grew. Many organizations were surprised to find just how narrow their band of profitable customers was, relative to their customer base.

Figure 7.6 represents a nonmaster's view of profitability. The view is an aggregate and offers little information for surgical initiatives.

Most organizations agree that less than 20% of their current customers generate 80% or more of their total profitability. Many organizations who have implemented activity-based costing as part of their information competency found that less than 5% of their customers represented the majority of their total profitability.

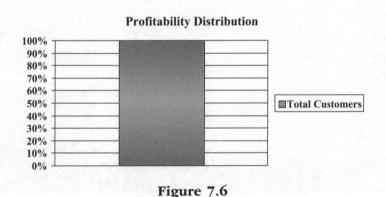

Figure 7.6

% of Customers vs. Monthly Profitability

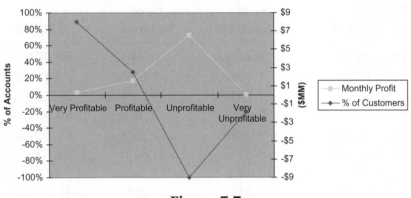

Figure 7.7

How well the organization understands its profitability can lead to new market opportunities. On the other hand, poor profitability measures can allow certain internal groups to cloak their poor business performance. One executive from a leading UK bank suggested that several groups within his organization developed great skill in hiding many poor financial and operational performances in their P&L because of the lack of detail and proper accountability.

Figure 7.7 shows a further evolution for a regional West Coast US bank on the road to mastery. The picture of profitability becomes clearer as well as the potential for decisive customer initiatives. From this detailed information, the organization can now target very specific customer segments for retention initiatives. They can also attempt to migrate these customers to higher levels of profitability.

Table 7.1 reveals a view closer to the mastery level with details revealing that only 0.19% of the customers were producing $3,021,332 out of $5,544,285 total profits. This small percent of customers shows just how vulnerable and dependent organizations are upon these customers.

Table 7.1

$ Profit/ HouseHold	% of HouseHold	% of Balance	$ Profit
Over $600	*0.19%*	*2.34%*	*$3,021,332*
$550 to 599	1.45%	1.53%	$945,321
$350 to 549	1.78%	4.22%	$1,353,798
$200 to 349	2.80%	9.35%	$4,354,323
$150 to 199	3.88%	7.55%	$3,456,387
$100 to 149	6.03%	31.87%	$2,435,678
$0 to 99	13.88%	12.44%	$978,453
–$1 to –25	22.34%	14.32%	–$7,345,234
–$26 to –49	33.78%	9.90%	–$2,453,654
–$50 to –74	13.64%	5.50%	–$877,954
Under –$75	0.23%	0.98%	–$324,165
Total	100.00%	100.00%	*$5,544,285*

Many organizations before they start the journey to information mastery find themselves expending tremendous resources beyond what is necessary because of their underlying weakness in the information on which they are basing their initiatives.

One leading US investment banking organization would send out a tremendous volume of mailings to its customers in hopes that a very small percentage of them would respond. The basic criteria were that the customers have a certain number of products and that they transacted at least five times a year with the organization. The executives were aware that many of the mail campaigns were indiscriminate yet they did not have an alternative because of their inherent information weakness.

As the organization progressed down the road to mastery, it was able to radically reduce the number of mailings while at the same time doubling their response rate.

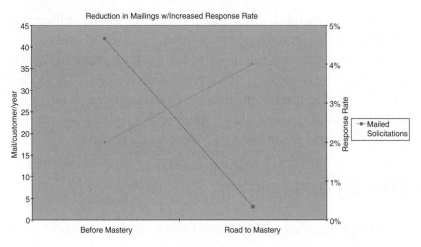

Figure 7.8

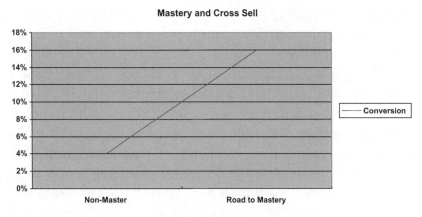

Figure 7.9

Before beginning the road to mastery, many organizations had the opportunity to cross-sell many products and services but lacked the information to do so. Even if they obtained the information, other missing elements of information competency such as cross-business-unit cooperation and incentives kept these very profitable initiatives from ever being launched.

One top UK bank found that when they had sufficiently developed information, cross-business-unit sharing, and leadership support, their ability to implement numerous and aggressive cross-selling initiatives skyrocketed. They also found that the added information perspectives from many business units caused the number of people who actually responded and purchased products to quadruple.

Mastery and risk

Most organizations do not have the information competency to accurately assess and then price for risk. Therefore, organizations typically under-price the risky business and over-price the less risky business. They also avoid very profitable business, which may be inherently risky yet could be priced appropriately for the risk with the appropriate level of information competency.

One leading UK bank was avoiding writing certain loans because they couldn't price them accurately for the level of risk. After they began to develop their information competency, they were able to write higher-risk loans without increasing the percentage of loans that went bad.

One very aggressive US insurance company found itself avoiding the traditional high-risk segments of car insurance, which was consistent with the industry as a whole. As this organization developed its information competency, it was able to aggressively target a segment of high-risk insurance which had been ostracized by its industry. It is now one of the largest sellers of car insurance in the industry with performance rates similar to companies insuring a lower risk pool.

Information mastery and marketing

Most of the organizations are able to obtain marketing response rates of 1–3%. Organizations who begin to lift their information competency achieve consistent lifts of 5–7% above industry norms. Organizations near mastery levels were able to consistently achieve 8–12% lifts above industry norms.

Information mastery and customer retention

For information masters, retaining the right customers is an inherent by-product of a deep understanding of customers and markets, not an initiative. This understanding and facility with customers comes from a deep and broad information competency. Companies report that as they travel the road of mastery, they are able to steadily ratchet down their customer churn levels.

One large East Coast US bank depicted in Figure 7.11 found that they were able to reduce churn rates each year by at least 0.5% relative to a current 6% churn rate. The organization did this by comparing economic cycles and customer behavior with appropriate product and services

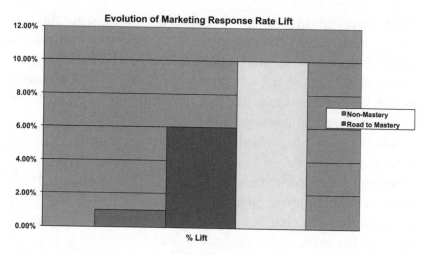

Figure 7.10

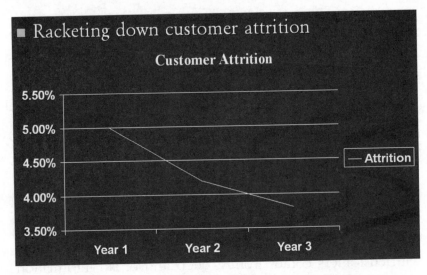

Figure 7.11

offerings. In doing so, they stopped a steady decline in good customers, while evolving moderately profitable customers into solidly profitable customers.

Information mastery and distribution channel effectiveness

Most organizations, before they began their road to competency, had distribution channels that operated with little knowledge of individual effectiveness and efficiency. In addition, as radical market changes caused radical changes in distribution channels, understanding the effect on customers was largely guesswork.

After developing further competencies, one leading Australian bank was able to reduce its channels by 20% and increase sales concurrently by 3%. This resulted from knowing the intimate interactions each customer had with each distribution channel and then fine-tuning these interactions to optimize value and profitability.

Information mastery and productivity

As companies improve their information competency levels, they spend more of their productive time in information-related activities. When a business can significantly reduce the time it takes to execute these activities, it can either:

1. execute more business programs; or
2. execute the same business programs with less resources.

If a business looks at how its time is spread between activities before the road to mastery, the mix is as follows:*

As Figure 7.12 depicts, 30% of employees' time is spent on vacation and personal time. The remaining 70% of employees' time is information-centric.

Business can be thought of as a series of decisions. If an organization can speed up decisions and the elements of making those decisions, productivity gains proliferate. In addition, the actual time spent in value-added activities becomes more productive. More advanced competency businesses report productivity gains in some areas measuring 10 times more compared to lower competency levels.

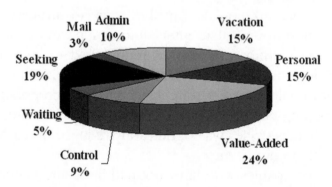

Figure 7.12

*Source: PA Consulting Group.

As companies evolve their competencies on the road to mastery, their productivity rises significantly because the amount of time spent in control, waiting, seeking, mail, and administration become less. A typical organization's allocation of time spent evolved to significantly higher value-added work time as Figure 7.12 depicts.

Information masters do more with less – Work Value

One of the most compelling but least talked about areas of information mastery is the ability of organizations to supplant workers. It has long been thought that the age of automation was over. "We have automated all the things we were able to with technology" is a belief often verbalized. We did that in the 60s and 70s. In fact, information mastery gives us another level of automation. Companies have found that the employee time and resources required to find, extract, understand, and apply information for business in their current information environment is many times more than that in a near mastery organization.

"Faster, better, cheaper" can only be successfully applied when a organization is on the road to mastery. One organization found that after automation, most of their marketing workforce could be redeployed or reduced.

One leading US investment banking organization found that they could redeploy roughly 45% of their corporate staff in marketing, sales, and service because the time required to complete activities was significantly reduced under higher information competency.

Many companies who have not had first hand experience with the impacts on efficiency are skeptical of the tremendous productivity improvements. Disbelievers are quickly convinced once they see the operational changes a systemic information competency has on an employee's time spent in accomplishing tasks. The improvement flows from the employees whose jobs depend on information to accomplish their objective gives them more time for pure value-added work. Much of this improvement is in cycle time reduction.

Another impact of information competency on employee productivity is properly aligning the right level of information-related work with the right level of employee. As discussed earlier, information-related work represents almost 90% of the employee's productive time.

Figure 7.13 depicts a director in a large US bank prior to transforming their information competencies. This director spent 25% of the time with information-related activities that were efficient for creating maximum added value for their position. The director ends up doing lower-level work and not creating level-appropriate value or decisions. For example, the director spends time working with analyst-level information in order to make director-level decisions.

While from a cost-effectiveness perspective, the inefficiencies of information work at inappropriate levels quickly add up, the market opportunity costs from the director not

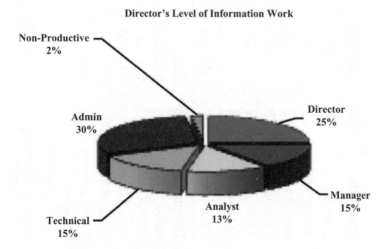

Director's Level of Information Work

Non-Productive 2%

Admin 30%

Director 25%

Manager 15%

Analyst 13%

Technical 15%

Figure 7.13

Table 7.2

Position	FTE's	Dir.Work	Mgr.Work	Anal.Work	Tech.Work	Admin.Work	Non-Prod.Work
Director	3	25%	15%	13%	15%	30%	2%
Manager	7	2%	32%	30%	10%	23%	3%
Analyst	12	0%	5%	37%	56%	1%	1%
Technical	8	0%	1%	2%	67%	28%	2%
Admin	4	0%	0%	0%	0%	88%	12%
TOTAL	34						

Position	FTE's	Dir.Work	Mgr.Work	Anal.Work	Tech.Work	Admin.Work	Non-Prod.Work
Director	38	25%	15%	13%	15%	30%	2%
Salary Level		$125,000	$95,000	$75,000	$65,000	$25,000	$125,000
Actual Cost		$31,250	$18,750	$16,250	$18,750	$37,500	$2,500
Cost Level		$31,250	$14,250	$9,750	$9,750	$7,500	$2,500
Cost of Time		$0	$4,500	$6,500	$9,000	$30,000	$0
% of Overpay		0%	32%	67%	92%	400%	0%
Cost of Time x FTE		$0	$171,000	$247,000	$342,000	$1,140,000	$0
Cost Ineffeciency	$1,900,000						

Table 7.3

Position	FTE's	Dir.Work	Mgr.Work	Anal.Work	Tech.Work	Admin.Work	Non-Prod.Work
Director	3	65%	10%	6%	9%	8%	2%
Manager	7	2%	32%	30%	10%	23%	3%
Analyst	12	0%	5%	37%	56%	1%	1%
Technical	8	0%	1%	2%	67%	28%	2%
Admin	4	0%	0%	0%	0%	88%	12%
TOTAL	34						

Position	FTE's	Dir.Work	Mgr.Work	Anal.Work	Tech.Work	Admin.Work	Non-Prod.Work
Director	38	65%	10%	6%	9%	8%	2%
Salary Level		$125,000	$95,000	$75,000	$65,000	$25,000	$125,000
Actual Cost		$81,250	$12,500	$7,500	$11,250	$10,000	$2,500
Cost Level		$81,250	$9,500	$4,500	$5,850	$2,000	$2,500
Cost of Time		$0	$3,000	$3,000	$5,400	$8,000	$0
% of Overpay		0%	32%	67%	92%	400%	0%
Cost of Time x FTE		$0	$114,000	$114,000	$205,200	$304,000	$0
Cost Inefficiency		$737,200					

operating at appropriate levels far exceeded the raw cost inefficiencies. Table 7.2 illustrates the annual cost inefficiencies from a director-level employee spending most of their time working at lesser skill levels within an organization.

As this organization developed its information competency, there was a significant shift in level-appropriate work for information-related activities, as can be seen from Table 7.3.

The annual cost saving was over one million dollars with estimated revenue opportunity cost savings estimated as three to five times those cost savings.

These examples show that the importance for a business to be master of their information and data sources can not be overemphasized. In periods of boom and bust, those companies with the highest level of mastery will be the ones who continue to prosper.

8 Managing the Employee Factor through Cycles

The Service Profit Chain is a well-known description of the inter-relationship of three elements of classic behavioral business cycle: happy employees tend to create happy customers, which positively affect share price and profitability.

There is indeed a strong correlation between employee fulfillment, customer fulfillment, and fluctuations in share price. The chart below (Figure 8.1) illustrates this powerful cause and effect relationship. The trend-line for share price has been manually shifted to the left on the chart by one quarter to more easily illustrate the relationships without the inevitable lag between customer fulfillment and share price fluctuations. In this particular example, the lag time between customer fulfillment changes and share price fluctuations was ¼. This can be a short as one week and as long as several quarters depending on how fast the market changes, e.g. sales cycles, speed of competitors.

This particular telecommunications organization actively tracked employee and customer satisfaction for two to three years using quarterly summary measurements. The correlation between customer satisfaction and employee satisfaction was 75 during eight measurement periods. The correlation was stronger than coincidental while the conclusions were intuitive and statistical. The study covered six business units that contained 75,000–80,000 employees.

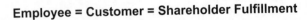

Employee = Customer = Shareholder Fulfillment

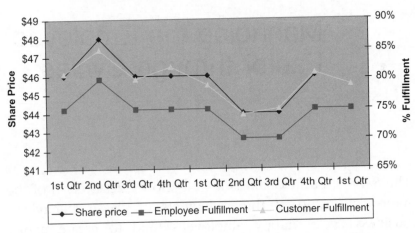

Figure 8.1

Actual responses for the employee survey totaled roughly 50,000 employees. The number of customers who responded from the six business units totaled 50–75 large corporate customers.

The element the Service Profit Chain does not overtly mention is leadership. It is after all the driving force behind employee fulfillment and never more than in challenging economic times.

In a nutshell: Effective human leadership begins with an understanding of the strengths and weaknesses of the leader themselves. From there, knowledge of the marketplace and the dynamics of human interaction in that marketplace enable the selection of the right people to fulfill customers. Developing those carefully selected people with care and providing them the freedom to be the best they can be for themselves and their customers is an essential element of human leadership. For both employee development and the execution of business objectives, an environment needs to be created where employees feel clearly directed and unquestionably empowered with responsibility and authority to fulfill customers as people. The nourishment of this environment centers on the employee's need for acknowledgment, respect, and trust. When these three essential human needs are fulfilled, employees will perform in extraordinary ways with customers responding in kind.

Like so many things in life and particularly in business, the idea sounds clear and simple. The challenge is in the doing. Let's take a look at some of the key elements to effective People Leadership regardless of the economic cycle.

By nature, most employees want to do a good job and many want to do a great job. One of the keys to improving the probability that they will do a good and even great job is to believe in them. Belief in employees will put them on the road to accomplish extraordinary things for themselves, the business, and ultimately the customer. As well as performing well at their jobs, they want to lead meaningful lives. Leaders can help them be excited, happy, and productive by showing them how their lives will be better and how the company will be better.

There are certain requirements for creating true employee fulfillment. Contrary to popular belief, what creates fulfilled employees is not predominantly the size of their paycheck but rather it is the feeling of acknowledgment, respect, and trust – the same human emotions needed by customers. In practical terms, it comes down to knowing what's expected of them, being supported to actually accomplish what is expected of them, having the abilities to accomplish them, and doing it all in a socially rewarding environment:

1. Understanding the objectives
2. Having support in accomplishing the objectives

3. Having the ability to accomplish the objectives
4. Healthy, interpersonal relationships at work.

Understanding the objectives

Communicate objectives – knowing the objectives is critical to any employee who has a desire to do a good job. Without knowing the goals, the employee is severely hampered from deriving esteem from completed tasks. The linkage is: understand objectives – complete task – derive self-esteem.

Help employees understand the "why" behind objectives

Many businesses create business strategies and objectives that are never fully explained to employees and still expect employees to execute these with passion and conviction. The chances of success in this scenario are minimal.

For example, if a business sets its objectives to sell premium products at premium prices without educating its employees as to why these prices are premium but still fair and a good value to customers, the ability to achieve these premium prices will be lessened. Helping employees to help customers understand pricing models is key to most business objectives yet it is a typical downfall for many businesses that believe the subject is somehow taboo and needs to remain a mystery to employees. Businesses need to explicitly communicate the pricing model to employees for their own understanding as well as enabling them to communicate with customers effectively.

A good example of this is Dorothy Lane Markets (DLM) who has strategically placed itself on the higher end of the grocery market with many specialized items at slightly higher prices than competitors. DLM's "boss", Norman Mayne spends a good deal of time educating his employees about the added value customers will experience by paying slightly higher prices for DLM's exceptional customer service and specialized products. It is important that the employees understand why these premium prices exist and that they are comfortable communicating the logic to customers. This is especially important when so many of Norman's competitors are promising to deliver the impossible – the cheapest prices, the best service, and the best quality. In reality, delivering all of these three promises is virtually impossible. A business can typically only achieve two out of three of these promises. Norman's focus has several core value dimensions.

The first is that DLM is reasonably competitive with other discount retailers on household brand items, e.g. Tide, Clorox, Charmin. This is a message that needs to be proactively communicated to customers to avoid the stereotyping that all of their products are higher margined and specialized. The second dimension is that DLM will always provide an exceptional level of humanizing customer service. This added level of customer service must be funded by additional margin in some aspect of the business. Norman jokingly comments that if DLM chose to have similar service and prices as their competitors it could easily be achieved by "simply laying off 40% of our workforce". The third is that he provides specialized products that justify slightly higher prices. DLM does command a premium price for such items as hand picked specialty olive oils imported directly from Italy. Developing this specialized product repertoire does require added investment and therefore added prices.

Norman must first educate his employees in a fair amount of detail about the reasons for these value dimensions. To understand these value dimensions, the investment and resources behind developing the specialty products must be understood. Every year, DLM sends seven or eight employees to Italy and France to research and select special food items that the team feels the customers would value and, as a result, would be happy to pay for the extra value. DLM's cheesemonger regularly travels to Switzerland to select fine cheeses for their cheese departments. Norman also funded a trip for the associate who runs DLM's meat departments to a little town in Italy to work alongside the Italian butchers to learn about creative ways to cut as well as combine different meats. DLM's meat manager has applied this learning by offering customers a specialized blend of breast of veal, sausage, poultry products, and select spices wrapped in Panchetta to create a wonderful new product. This cooperative working arrangement with other European butcher shops came about from a previous trip in which a DLM employee noticed how beautifully one Italian butcher shop's meat was displayed – "The meat looked like diamonds displayed in the case".

Another good example of DLM's highly valued specialty items is their ultimate pursuit of the finest virgin olive oil from estates in Italy's Tuscan region. Offering their customers the finest virgin olive oils can be contrasted with their competitors' offerings of olive oil in bulk from places where the olive oil is mixed and blended in varying degrees of quality. For DLM's fruit spreads, Norman provides his customers with exceptionally healthy fruit spreads without adding sugar. Employees are educated about the quality of their fruit spreads by actually being sent to the processing plant to watch the fruit spreads being created. These specialty items are typically branded as special DLM products. DLM also provides Coleman's natural beef, which comes from cattle raised from birth without antibiotics nor added growth-stimulating hormones, and being given feed that is free of pesticide residues. In addition, because there is no growth-stimulating hormone added, the cattle take longer to "finish", i.e. develop more naturally and slowly from conception to steer. This more natural process costs more but is healthier than cattle raised "fast" and mass-produced using drugs to speed up the animal's growth.

In addition, this specialty beef is not cut with a meat saw, as most beef is, but is cut by hand by DLM's trained butchers. Norman's deli manager has stopped buying most of the national brands of lunchmeat and has switched almost exclusively to buying Boar's Head delicatessen products. Boar's Head products are still made the old fashioned way without the use of artificial colors or artificial flavors, extenders, or fillers, which other delicatessen manufacturers discovered make products appear better than they really are. As a result, the cost of this lunchmeat is higher and a certain segment of DLM customers are willing to pay more because they value a healthy delicatessen product.

Norman also sent their head baker to France to learn how the French make their breads in order to enhance DLM's bakery selection. On a recent trip to France by DLM's baker, they bought a $70,000 Paviller oven. Six months after the purchase, two people flew over from France to build this special oven in one of DLM's stores. One of the unique features of this European oven is that opening the doors causes only a two-degree loss of heat, whereas a typical American baking oven loses roughly 40 degrees of heat. Heat loss during baking significantly changes the process of baking fine breads. This specialized oven allows DLM to bake great breads in their store that the customers value highly. As a result of having the oven, they sold more French baguettes than they did of the popular household brand Wonder bread. DLM also prepares its own salad makings for its deli rather than taking the typical path of buying salad makings from a factory. In the prepared food sections, the chefs only use real butter or clarified butter, not margarine. Norman also uses their fine DLM Tuscan virgin olive oils in their prepared foods rather than factory processed olive oils.

These specialized DLM products are never aggressively marketed to customers but simply displayed alongside other household brand grocery items. The customers make the determination whether DLM's specialty products warrant the slight price premium.

When employees understand the value clearly they can communicate it to customers. When the customers understand the value clearly, they have no problem paying slightly extra.

Promote understanding objectives by employee involvement in planning

A fundamental weakness of many companies' strategic planning process and the resulting strategic plan is the fact that most employees feel little or no involvement in a plan only communicated to them after the fact. It is critical that a company create a planning process that not only helps employees understand the resulting objectives but also creates a "feeling" that they helped create the objectives themselves. As a result, they are more likely to believe that the vision is valid and therefore more likely to actually execute it.

Los Alamos National Bank's (LANB) strategic planning process brought involvement from internal organizations to create a strategic plan for six years from today that addresses future visions and possibilities. It is very difficult for an organization to execute a vision that is solely the idea of executives; however, there is tremendous buy-in from employees when they have had a part in the decision-making process because they then feel – "I helped shape that".

Having support in accomplishing the objectives

First, give employees both responsibility and authority. Only when they have both can they fulfill objectives. They will also act with increasing independence and creativity which will likely extend what both business and employee may have thought possible.

Secondly, provide them the right tools. This human desire is very much linked to self-esteem. If the right tools are unavailable to an employee, this directly affects his ability to take pride in a job well done, and thus feel satisfaction as a productive employee. 90% of what causes an employee to fail at his job is the lack of timely and accurate information. It is important to note that, statistically, having the right tools is more important to an employee than general happiness on the job. This has to do with self-esteem being a deeper and more powerful emotion than a general sense of happiness. In many cases, tools and materials rather than information are what are necessary to complete a job. However, it still holds true that these tools and materials must be accessible and in top working order for an employee to feel growth in self-esteem.

Tools also create the human expectation and competency for great results. Providing the right tools for employees has a multidimensional impact on employee esteem. At the front end, providing the employee with excellent tools increases their esteem because it makes them feel as though the employer cares enough about them as human beings to provide them with the best tools available. They also feel that by being given these great tools, their employer expects great results. Using these tools, they feel an inherent sense of pride and productivity. When they have completed tasks efficiently and effectively, they feel a tremendous sense of accomplishment and pride.

One telecommunications organization focused on the critical questions of how well they were supporting their employees in fulfilling their objectives. One critical question they asked their employees was: Do the services provided by our company make you more functional? They also drill down into this employee satisfaction analysis to determine which specific processes could potentially make the employees more confident or help them "feel" more confident, e.g. information systems, support infrastructure, human resource support infrastructure, and operational support infrastructure, such as payables. One of the processes they examined was the submission of a voucher, or a purchase order. Then they analyzed how these processes could be made more user-friendly and less onerous. They also analyzed how an increase in web utilization could add to the ease of managing human resource issues, e.g. being able to update personnel records online. One way to improve employee job satisfaction through operational efficiencies was to enable HR personnel to submit vouchers or purchase orders online versus physically filling out a form, then faxing or sending it as an inner office memo. This focus on improving operational efficiencies through improving their company's customer support infrastructure enabled employees to achieve a higher likelihood of fulfilling customer needs, and therefore to feel a higher degree of self-esteem and social acceptance.

One challenge was to measure the return on the investment from the capital expenditures on the human resource systems to enable these online efficiencies. Another challenge was accounting for improvements in one area when the company had to transfer resources from another area whose process was previously manual. These however were manageable challenges as the return was clearly there. Another analysis focusing on investments made in employee satisfaction and the gross impact on retention of customers, and the resulting changes in the company's economic status and customer satisfaction, clearly showed the value in the investments made.

Having the ability to accomplish the objectives

A good example of this is the ability to respond to a customer in a timely fashion. Any human employee who is relating to a human customer is driven by social forces to either please them or garner acceptance from them. If an employee cannot respond in a timely manner to a customer request this highly motivating connection of social acceptance cannot be achieved and both customer and employee are left unsatisfied.

Healthy, interpersonal relationships at work

Employees need good personal relationships with people at work because that is how they derive much of their human satisfaction while at work, i.e. do I have a good friend at work?

Create "fun" at work

Regularly schedule "fun" activities to best enhance positive emotions and reduce negative emotions. Keeping associates happy in the pursuit of keeping customers happy requires activities that diffuse, release, and uplift associates' emotions. One fun and uplifting activity is a scooter contest that a WalMart store put on for its managers and associates. They began with all the associates, department managers, and store managers having coffee and donuts in the morning, and then they formed teams to scooter down the store aisles.

Other similar emotion-releasing games were contests in which associates competed by hula-hooping down the store aisle. Whoever could go the farthest would win a $25 gift certificate from the store. One WalMart store manager will announce a time for "zoning munchies" during more mundane activities, e.g. zoning (restocking shelves) or late-night store cleanup. Zoning munchies typically consists of candy that is handed out to help make the activity of cleaning up a store more fun particularly for the younger associates. These "zoning munchies" also boost the energy level of the associates.

Reduce employee unhappiness

Reducing employee unhappiness is just as important, if not more so, than focusing on enhancing employee happiness. It is best for the employee as well as business. The impact of unhappy employees on the interactions with customers as well as overall company image and brand is many times underestimated. Disgruntled employees are a major source of bad word-of-mouth information for customers. In most countries, a significant percentage of how a customer forms an opinion of the organization is how the company treats its employees. This makes sense because employees spend more time with the customers than the chairman or top-level management spend with customers.

Be proactive against "emotional burn-out"

Businesses that are insensitive to emotional burnout of employees pay a hidden price from the employee, other associates, and customers.

Allocate time, training, and space to help associates emotionally "recoup" from serving difficult customers. Sometimes, associates must engage in conversation with a customer who is venting some intense feelings. In a small percentage of cases, they will intentionally, or unintentionally, release their anger on store associates, which transfers that anger to the associate. The associate will then need an avenue to vent their anger or have a physical place removed from customers to go to cool down. In this scenario, the associate's frown will have to be "turned upside-down" as well. There are some truly frustrating situations for associates who are sincerely making every effort to give a customer the best advice or information but that customer instead expresses anger or disbelief that the associate is acting on their behalf.

Sensitive employees become desensitized to common customer inquiries – employees whose job it is to respond to customer inquiries often get desensitized due to the repetitiveness of customer inquiries and questions. It is easy for call center employees to appear uncaring because they have heard the same question several hundred times that week. What is a boring, repetitive question to the call center, has many times created significant anxiety for the customer. The customer's problem may be something they will only deal with once in a lifetime and that often determines their emotional reaction.

Create emotional "time and space" for employees besieged by stress from aggressive management, "unkind" customers, and operational issues. Two realities of a customer oriented business are that:

1. Some customers are unkind.
2. Employees have an emotional limit to what they are able to endure.

The general manager of one Land Rover Center has observed that there will always be a certain segment of the population who are never satisfied and these customers can cause significant morale damage to any employee with their behavior. As a natural aspect of human emotions, when one person is unkind to another person, the negative feelings created must have some avenue for venting. Otherwise, there is a likelihood that the employee may transfer or vent those negative emotions to either another customer or another employee, perpetuating the negative emotional cycle. An environment that makes it "okay" to take time away from business to resolve negative emotions is the key to stopping the negative emotional cycle.

In one example, a gentleman entered a WalMart store responding to an ad in the previous day's newspaper for a special on futons. The gentleman came to the WalMart store to purchase the futon and found that they were out of stock for the sale. He was very angry and aggressively approached the manager. These out-of-stock situations occasionally occur because WalMart is reliant on local vendors to supply the right goods, at the right time, and at the right place. The manager did a product search using WalMart's item locator, which scans a 150-mile radius to find which stores have a particular item in stock. The manager found that no store within a 150-mile radius had these futons in stock, so she told the customer that the best thing that she could do for him at that time was to issue him a rain check for the sale price of the futon. He refused to believe that this was the best that could be done to solve the situation, even though he actually witnessed the manager perform the item locator function and saw the actual results of the search. The customer continued insisting that he wanted the futon "right there, right then". He was very angry, unreasonable, and rude. Continuing her best efforts to be courteous and friendly the manager offered the customer an additional 10% discount off the sale price. Eventually, though still unsatisfied, the disgruntled customer grudgingly accepted the rain check with the 10% additional discount. Maintaining a "good attitude" is often a challenge for managers and associates. In this case, the manager took some time to remember the many positive and humanly rewarding experiences she had in her job to help put this negative in perspective.

Arcona Devan, owner of The Arcona Studio, an exclusive health spa in Los Angeles, California, observed that when her employees interact with the occasional negative client, they absorb a portion of that client's negative emotions. When they absorb too much negative emotion, e.g. tension, anger, they deplete themselves and quickly become unproductive. To overcome this, Arcola applies the principle of chakras and the directional flow of personal and universal energies to keep both her employees and clients happy. She encourages her employees to visualize the positive emotions or energies that they give to their clients as not being their own but coming from inexhaustible universal energies. Her employees are encouraged to visualize pulling energies in one direction from the universe, through their crown chakra (head) and pushing the energy into the client. When employees visualize "giving" to their clients in this manner, they feel they can give more to clients for a longer period of time because they are not depleting their own energies. They also are not absorbing negative energies because the energy flow is only in one direction. While these principles may seem too ethereal for mainstream business, emotional burnout of employees is common for employees in roles that serve customers who have a steady stream of negative comments or reactions. Burnout has a significant impact on employee productivity and customer fulfillment. Experimenting with more innovative approaches such as these may be worthwhile in high employee burnout environments such as call centers and customer service operations.

It starts and ends with communication

The common thread in all the above illustrations is communication. Good communication can help a business ride any storm; poor communication can cause disasters to occur when there wasn't even a problem (mountains from molehills as it were). During downturn markets the role of communication expands even further.

Consider a large corporation with customer-facing employees who likely work nowhere near the corporate headquarters, seldom if ever see a senior executive, see any level of management maybe once a month, and whose main source of internal communication is short emails, notes, or word-of-mouth from other employees. Now consider that these same employees are talking with their customers all day long every day and those customers are getting concerned about the economy and about losing their jobs and their homes. Who is the employee getting their view of the current situation from? Who are they going to empathize most with? That doesn't even include everything an employee is exposed to through news, media, and the Internet.

Particularly in downturns, there are two core messages that leadership needs to communicate:

1. Confidence about the company
2. Openness and honesty about the company's plans.

The second point cannot be overemphasized. Consciously or unconsciously people pick up with the leader feels and wants. Given the Harvard Communication research that found 58% of what we take away from verbal communication is nonverbal but rather comes from body language and energy, this is not surprising. So if a leader is worried about the economy and about losing their own job, they will not be effective in telling employees that everything is fine, and there's no need to worry.

Just as with customers there is a collective consciousness that can occur especially when individuals are inundated with stories of economic windfalls or disasters. Employees have at the best of times a natural concern about the job or rather their security that comes with the job. Thus, they also have a concern for the employing company. However, when an employee is fulfilled in their role, that concern is minimized to the point of almost disappearing. On the other hand, if the employee isn't completely fulfilled within the role, that concern can become a heightened level of anxiety and it can create unfounded future negative scenarios.

One large retail bank addressed these issues proactively during an economic downturn by having its CEO be more present and vocal in communicating their plans to address the downturn in business. The CEO also went on a major news network to share their plans how they would appropriately address the downturn. He did this with an openness and candor that was very credible and thus, he was able to build trust with customers and employees (and financial analysts). Another senior executive held more frequent employee sessions to proactively address concerns in a forthright manner and so reassure employees that the company was confident and well suited to address the downturn economy.

Even in small companies, there needs to be proactive communication to address even small changes that appear to be the harbinger of further potential "scary" changes in the company. One small consulting organization was making ordinary operational efficiency changes to their operations that concerned many of the employees. The CEO immediately addressed these changes as normal changes and reassured employees that this would not lead to further cuts in employees.

Create an open and honest culture before economic transitions occur

Change causes stress. Economic transitions are no different. These economic transitions create a chain of emotional and behavioral reactions that heighten the importance of an open and honest corporate culture:

* Change creates uncertainty
* Uncertainty creates anxiety
* Anxiety reduces trust.

It is this sequence of emotional and behavioral reactions that must be proactively addressed by the leadership and management of an organization. This makes regular, weekly "huddles" critical for communicating to employees the honest facts about the businesses direction and condition. When employees feel like they are "in the loop" and understand the thinking that is going on behind closed doors, when restructuring and downsizing are executed, they are better prepared to handle the additional changes.

One senior executive from a vacation destination business worked hard to create a culture of open and honest mediation between employees. When it came time to addressing the issues of a contracted economy, the straight talk of using phases like, "these are unprecedented times with difficult choices", did much to send the signal to the employees that the management team was being straightforward and open with them. It showed the employees that the management team respected them enough to communicate openly and honestly about the hard decisions ahead. Honesty creates trust. Silence creates fear and distrust. Employees who trust management are more productive. Employees who are fearful and distrusting experience a reduction in productivity. These feelings of fear and anxiety are compounded by a sense of "survivor guilt" by employees who are left after the layoffs. Having a culture of open and honest mediation also helps acknowledge these survivor guilt feelings and helps move employees on to a productive and forward looking path.

Even in challenging economic times, there is unwanted employee attrition. One of the keys to employee satisfaction and maintaining your desired workforce is this culture of openness and honesty. Despite popular belief that pay is the dominating factor, cultural attributes like respect, trust, and openness are equally if not more important.

One example is an employee working at a Best Buy retail store who was making over $17 an hour which was a strong wage for a retail store. He decided to leave that store in favor of working for Apple at one of their local Apple stores. While Apple offered him less money per hour, the respectful and open culture that predominated at the Apple store was the key to his decision to leave one employer for another. Not only was this person happier working at Apple, the linkage between happy employees and happy customers is significant. Statistically 80% of a customer's experience can be attributed to how the employee feels about their work and about how they are treated by their management. All these factors contribute to the fact that a corporate culture of openness and honesty is more important during transitional times than in stable economies.

Having an open and honest culture does not mean that you share all the proprietary and confidential information with everyone. It means that you share as much of it as you can that will have an impact on positive behavior.

In one travel business, the executive was open with his frontline management and asked them to think of ways they could lower operational costs for the business because the economy was affecting their forecasts. Without being asked, his two primary managers took the initiative to personally call all the major hotel companies that they worked with around the world to see what cost savings could be worked out with them. Their initiative resulted in several hundred thousand dollars in costs savings. This was not an executive delegated initiative; it was purely facilitated by a candid discussion that the company's forecast was in jeopardy by the weakened economy. The two managers presented the results of their work and the cost savings in a six-page presentation to the executive and his VP of Operations. The key here is that it was the culture that enabled the two managers to understand the economic conditions of the business, and have the freedom to act without having to wait for a specific cost initiative to be delegated. If this type of culture can exist in challenging economic times the opportunities are exponential for the same type of culture to be facilitated in prosperous economic times.

Manage the double-edged sword of employee stress

Economic cycles cause stress. Whether it is the flurry of business activity during economic expansions or the added uncertainty and constraints of a contracting economy, both customers and therefore employees experience more stress. This added stress is a double-edged sword particularly in contracting economies. On one hand, employees are more in fear of their jobs and may increase their effort to execute their tasks and responsibilities. On the other hand, they can be preoccupied by the added anxieties and become less productive, less creative, and less likely to deliver the best customer experience. They are also more likely to stay in jobs or positions that they are unhappy with but where they must stay for the "paycheck". This added stress is particularly detrimental to "high touch" businesses where the customer experience is critical. This compounds the inherent stress that already exists in industries with "built-in high" stress levels, e.g. the travel industry.

Inherently, the travel industry has high stress levels and challenges with employee morale for multiple dimensions. One significant factor is how the public treats the travel industry, particularly the airline carriers. This is compounded by the fact that it is very difficult for airline employees to leave their jobs, i.e. significant barriers to exit. The highly structured and organized labor organizations, e.g. Hotel Employees and Restaurant Employees Union (HERE), Association of Flight Attendants-CWA, Air Line Pilots Association (ALPA), International Association of Machinists (IAMAW), add to the structured nature of this industry. This has much to do with how the compensation structure is executed in the industry.

In many positions, if an employee leaves one company and starts with another company, they typically experience a severe reduction in pay. These economic barriers to the free movement of labor are compounded by the treatment of the public. From one perspective, the public has set the tone for their own customer experience by their transient attitude towards the industry's staff. Both of these dimensions are supercharged during periods of economic contraction.

Provisions must be made by these businesses to not only allow freer movement between jobs but also to ensure that there are job rotation policies into less stressful jobs. Coupling these factors with a confluence of major industry events, e.g. the 2001 9/11 attacks, concern in 2003 over SARS (Severe Acute Respiratory Syndrome), the 2007/08 oil price escalation, and economic contractions, only increase the necessity to treat employees as real human beings.

Manage your managers' perceived outlook

When economies transition toward contractions, many managers gravitate toward the "doom and gloom" persona. A contracted economy does require serious measures and with that comes added stress and concerns. When a management team circulates around a business with a negative outlook, it becomes contagious. In short order employees take on the same outlook, and productivity as well as customer relations are negatively impacted. This is why it is critical to coach the management team to keep a realistic, positive attitude and outlook with employees in the face of economic adversity.

One executive from the travel industry coached his management team from the beginning to focus on projecting a positive persona with employees. He did this both with his seasoned and new executives. He coached them that whether it is in the hallway, company kitchen, or just having an informal lunch, that they maintain a "can-do" attitude with all employees. He encouraged them to maintain in tough times, when those great leadership qualities were needed the most, the great leadership qualities that they exhibited in prosperous times. His coaching to his staff was that they were going to have many meetings about dealing with the tight economic conditions but once they left the meeting, they should make sure their attitudes were forward looking and positive. The other theme that he promoted was to encourage his management team to make sure the employees were taking care of themselves personally, particularly when business conditions created much higher stresses on them. His coaching included telling them to encourage the employees to continue their regular activities, particularly those that helped balance their business and personal life, e.g. regular workout routines, family activities, and time off.

Recognizing the management and employee power balance

For much of our remembered work history, it was an employers' market. However, the degree to which management have the power in the hiring process has started to fluctuate. Some of this was due to baby boomers moving out of the workforce, some was the different attitude towards work of the Generation Xs. Basically though, regardless of all the impacting factors, it's a supply and demand question.

This economy has seen a balance of power shift back to management because now there is an oversupply of employment and constriction in positions. Just as with customers there's a downside to making quick sales instead of spending the time to invest in relationships and build trust, so with employees it's critical to spend the time to get (and to keep) the best employees for the company and for the customer.

Employees are the lifeblood of the company. When economies contract, it's a critical decision point as to what is the best path to try to reduce employee expenses. What is the best path?

As was well articulated in *As Layoffs Spread, Innovative Alternatives May Soften the Blow** premature layoffs can be a disaster.

*Published November 26, 2008 in Knowledge@Wharton.

Any scenario involving layoffs negatively impacts the remaining employees which invariably impacts productivity. And if insufficient employees are laid off and the recession continues, the impact to the company's bottom line might not be sufficient to realize any benefit from the initial layoffs. And if the economy starts to recover quicker than expected, the company could be left understaffed to meet the challenge.

Rather than go straight to layoffs, some consider alternatives, such as:

- voluntary retirements
- salary cuts
- hiring freezes
- reductions of hours
- changes in benefits and expense policies.

Spreading the pain

The costs of layoffs go beyond the morale problems they cause – both for those laid off and those who keep their jobs. Unemployment insurance premiums spike. Depending on the company, there are severance packages to consider and outplacement services (costly in these days of bigger demand for them). Litigation is a not insignificant risk. In addition a company faces "start-up costs" once the economy starts to move to recovery.

On the other hand, there's nothing like a good economic downturn to get rid of dead wood. A sagging economy can be an opportune time for management to deal with performance problems by using the bluntest instrument possible. Firing people is often difficult to execute, but an overarching justification (like an economic downturn) tends to lessen complications in doing so.

Conventional wisdom is that the smaller the company, the more apt owners are to work things out personally with workers. "We recently reduced hours in our department," says Ben Atkinson, director of risk management for Edison, N.J.-based Peoplelink Staffing, a provider of staffing, software training, consulting, development, and support. "My team proposed the idea, and each [of us] volunteered to reduce [his or her] number of work days. I have asked other managers across our enterprise to consider this approach."

Atkinson says the move has prevented major disruptions to projects, and retains the investment the company has made in training its employees. "This is not to say we won't consider layoffs," he adds. "But it depends on your economic prognosis. If we anticipate a recovery sooner, we are more likely to consider reduced hours. If we expect a long slog, layoffs may seem more appropriate."

Smaller private companies are more personal as all employees tend to know and have relationships with all other employees (including the CEO). These companies also do not have as much pressure to cut costs if the owner believes it is possible to ride out the storm. Conversely, in a publicly held company, even if a CEO is inclined to seek alternatives to layoffs, pressure from shareholders and Wall Street analysts to cut staff might be too great.

In the past 20 years, staff cutbacks have more frequently included attractive incentives, according to Daniel O'Meara, a senior fellow at Wharton's Human Resources Center and an employment law attorney with Montgomery, McCracken, Walker & Rhoads in Philadelphia. In the 1990s, O'Meara saw more opportunities for voluntary retirement incentives. "It was more feasible with a defined benefit plan, and very feasible with overfunded pension plans. If [employers] could afford it now, it might be that anyone with 20 years of service and at least 55 [years old] would be treated as [if they have] 30 years [of service] and ... are 65."

These days, such options are less generous, he says, citing a particular hospital where buyout offers are more typical: one or two weeks of pay for each year of service. "No one who is happy in their job and doesn't have something lined up would leave for four or eight weeks of pay. But you might have people who were going to leave anyway, and see it as a great opportunity."

The other side of that coin is that some companies make such offers "only to show employees that they are basically good people, just before the involuntary layoffs come. Since the Depression, all these alternatives have been discussed – to lay people off or share the pain," O'Meara says, recalling personal experiences as a young man growing up in western Pennsylvania, where he worked summers in a steel mill. "There, when things got slow, we all worked four days a week. That's [a case] where the union had the effect of making sure people held on to their jobs. A lot of this stuff has been around for a long time. These decisions have huge impacts on people and there are no easy solutions."

Avoiding layoffs "at all costs"

"The economy has got us all watching very closely. Like anyone, we are trying to figure out where the bottom is," says Tim Roth, president of Megavolt, an agricultural machine re-manufacturer based in Springfield, Mo. "Agriculture has been relatively strong compared to other industries, but in June, we saw that in future months we would have some problems. We tried to figure out how to keep people and avoid layoffs at all costs."

Megavolt has two advantages over many other private companies. First, it is a joint venture with two other organizations descended from International Harvester after a buyout 25 years ago. In some cases, this allows employees who get additional training and certification to temporarily move to other work places, as needed.

Second, the company moved in October to a "shared work program" of three 10-hour days a week as a way to cope with the downturn. While workers keep their jobs, the lost 10 hours each week is nonetheless enough for them to be eligible for state unemployment benefits in Missouri, where Megavolt is located. The Missouri program also does not restrict unemployment benefits for people who take on part-time jobs, Roth says. And within the shared work program, companies can soften the blow to people who are laid off. In that situation, the state stipulates that the employer give the volunteers a specific recall date – generally, anywhere from one to six months out, according to Roth. The company also maintains health benefits for employees and defers their contribution to the premiums. "It's one thing to have lost a job completely, but it's quite another to be able to look for work and know you have got something else behind you," Roth says. "It's a good program."

In the end, companies need to balance what's best for their employees while making sure the company remains viable in tough times.

For example: Cisco Systems in 2001, after the tech bubble and before 9/11, allowed employees to take sabbaticals while they were paid one-third their salary. "The reason was that at one-third pay, you couldn't survive forever, but it was enough money that you wouldn't necessarily be looking for another job" in the meantime. Cisco saved both money and talent.

Managing a fast recovery

During economic contraction and recession, even if busi-nesses use these alternative strategies they might still have significant layoffs. In addition, they have reduced their production capabilities. If the economy recovers quickly, the biggest challenge will be to manage the quality of output because you have hired people quickly who are still in the learning mode.

Use downturn times to train

By increasing the amount of training remaining employees receive during slow economic periods; a business can reduce the "catch-up" time needed with a recovery (and the potential hiring and rehiring of employees).

Recognizing the mentoring of new employees

Another initiative that can add value in speeding up a new employee's time to full productivity is mentorship.

A large bank in Canada recently relaunched their recognition of the importance of mentorship of new employees. This recognition is important in any economy: it is particularly important in recovery and prosperous times where employment is plentiful.

The cost of a new employee is significant for any business. The new employee will require at least two hours a day initially of supervision by a senior member of the staff. They will also require roughly two weeks of one-to-one mentoring on the job. In addition, the first month where they are working on their own will still require many questions being answered by someone who is experienced. This first month also is a period where many mistakes are being made which puts pressure on the new employee as well as other coworkers. All of this additional help takes resources. This is why it is critical to reward the people who are helping new employees because typically this type of mentoring activity goes unrewarded and leads to feelings of resentment and lack of acknowledgment.

Mentoring is a critical activity for any business because most new employees are likely to leave within the first year. For a ballpark figure, $5,000 per new employee is the additional cost incurred by the business to acquire them. This $5,000 does not include training of the employee. This type of mentoring recognition increases employee satisfaction, customer service levels, general morale, and long-term business growth. Conversely, high employee turnover has the opposite effect on all these critical elements of business success.

In good times and in bad

Employees have a direct impact on customers. And customers have a direct impact on any company's bottom line. In good times (and more so, in bad), the employee factor is a crucial component to any business's success.

Ensuring leaders are focused on creating and maintaining a positive culture with open, honest communication regardless of the economic cycle will go a long way to ensuring the long-term prosperity of a business. Take a long-term view of your most important asset – your employees.

Leveraging the Power of the Community (Physical and Online)

Community has in recent years made a resurgence in its importance in people's lives. These is due to many factors:

- the global warming and group focus on trying to take better care of the environment;
- the increased connectivity of countries;
- the economic slowdown's global impact; and
- the increasing move to reprioritization of values by governments, businesses, and individuals.

It is typical in times of economic slowdown to return somewhat to "the basics". For individuals to need to rely more on community – whether it be the homeless supporting each other in shanty Hooverville towns during the Great Depression, FDR's New Deal, or the current stimulus packages of numerous countries.

The difference this time is the Internet. It takes the phrase "It's a small world" to a whole new level of meaning. It has also become a virtual community that in many ways rivals the "real" world.

Both the physical community and the virtual community have a role to play during boom and bust economic cycles.

The physical community

While during boom periods, businesses may not need to look for partners and additional support, during bust periods all avenues need to be explored. One such avenue that should not be overlooked (especially by small businesses) is that of community support.

This can come from nonprofit organizations, other for-profit businesses, and from various levels of local government. Whether a boom or a bust economic cycle, there is no downside to leveraging the local government business development and retention programs. During economic transitions and downturns, there are many local and national business development programs that are set up to assist businesses in retaining and developing customers and prospects.

To give a better understanding of what types of services are likely available for businesses, a region in Canada currently has the Hants Regional Development Authority (Hants RDA). The Hants Regional Development Authority is a forward looking organization established to support and advance community economic development in Hants County in Nova Scotia, Canada. The Hants RDA works with businesses, community groups, and all three levels of government to champion the interests of Hants County locally, regionally, and internationally. While this organization is primarily set up to help retain and expand its activity in the region, its resources are relevant to a business's customer management challenges in economic transitions.

One of Hants RDA's primary community-based economic development strategies is a focus on "taking care of, nurturing and supporting" existing businesses. This strategy is based on face-to-face interactions to understand the challenges, needs, and opportunities of each individual business and then working with the businesses to tackle obstacles and unlock opportunities to business growth. While one of their primary goals is to keep businesses from relocating to other areas, it is also set up to help businesses survive and prosper in economically challenged environments.

The process begins when the Hants RDA's Account Executive requests a one to two-hour site visit interview with an executive of the company, e.g. the President, CEO, owner, or manager to introduce the Hants RDA's business retention and expansion program (BR+E) through a site visit. Before the visit, an account executive will have thoroughly researched the company. Some background information will be conorganizationed, but the discussion will focus on challenges and opportunities facing the company. In addition to the interview, the account executive may request a short facility tour, if appropriate. After each interview, the account executive records a summary of the discussion in a confidential database. This database tracks follow-up with each company and allows the creation of reports on community-wide business trends (without naming any companies).

Local Action Teams work with employers to develop immediate solutions and long-term strategies that support business growth. Action Team members have the resources and experience to effectively identify, review, and act on issues affecting local business in areas such as:

- accessing new customer markets
- recruiting skilled employees
- addressing training needs
- addressing business location and relocation needs
- accessing financing information
- assisting with local government.

All of these activities have significant impact on customer management and the particular dynamics of the economic transition or challenge.

The Hants RDA also partners with a group of other public organizations geared to supporting businesses challenged with changing economic conditions:

- Annapolis Valley Work Activity Society
- CBDC Hants-Kings
- East Hants & District Chamber of Commerce
- Futureworx Job Search Centre
- Hantport & Area Business Association
- Job Resource Centre
- Municipality of East Hants
- Municipality of West Hants
- Nova Scotia Community College
- The Women in Business Initiative
- Town of Hantsport
- Town of Windsor
- West Hants Chamber of Commerce.

Minas Basin Pulp and Power

While the major upheaval of the US financial institutions sent shockwaves through the global economy in 2009, the CEO of one of Nova Scotia's oldest companies was starting to see the light of day from his previous business efforts. For more than a year, their CEO (Scott Travers), of Minas Basin Pulp and Power, had been steering the Hantsport paperboard manufacturer through a perfect storm of rising input costs. Not only were energy prices surging, but the world price of old corrugated cardboard (OCC), the material Minas Basin uses to make its product, was skyrocketing because of the soaring demand from the Asian economies. "We were fighting our darkest days when the rest of the world was enjoying unparalleled economic growth," says Travers. But in the face of adverse economic conditions, the business turned to innovative supply alternatives. The CEO realized that he could never be competitive with his current customers given the current escalating supply costs. Minas Basin countered rising energy costs by investing even more heavily in sustainable energy including biomass cogeneration, wind energy, and tidal energy. Minas Basin rose to the challenge of climate change by becoming one of the first Canadian companies to trade carbon credits.

When the US economy struggled, driving commodity and energy prices down, Minas Basin's fortunes started to change. "We saw the prices of our biggest inputs – energy and OCC, fall dramatically," Travers says. Like many businesses, Minas Basin has not emerged from the negative economic transition unscathed. They were forced to temporarily shut down operations toward the end of last year, and Travers warns that an economic slowdown may affect demand for their product. But the experience illustrates the complexities of managing customers in a global economy, and just how difficult it is to predict what the impact of the US economic downturns will be on other countries' local economies.

"A slowdown is never good news," says Ryan MacNeil, Executive Director of the Hants RDA. "But even in the middle of a downturn, there are always opportunities for growth."

For instance, in a January press conference, Minas Basin announced a number of advances on its estimated $12 million Bay of Fundy tidal energy facility. When it comes on stream, the project will be North America's first tidal energy project. Together with Nova Scotia Energy Minister Barry Barnet, Travers made a number of announcements including new technology, the location of the turbines, and an upcoming construction contract. The Bay of Fundy has the capacity to power as many as 100,000 homes, according to energy department statistics.

Ryan MacNeil says Minas Basin is a classic example of the benefits of diversification. "After 82 years in business Minas Basin has a lot to teach us in terms of staying power," MacNeil says. Having diverse interests in the paper and energy industries has helped "storm harden" the company, MacNeil says, allowing it to thrive, even in times of economic hardship.

For Travers, the keys to successfully steering a company through a downturn include holding a line on costs, but also looking through adversity to the underlying opportunity. "As a manager, you need to get creative and closely examine all the opportunities in front of you," he says. "That's true whether you launched your company last year or last century."*

The web community

We're at a historic turning point. We have an economy going bust, which leads to greater insecurity within consumers. This in turn leads to an increased desire (and need) for control. At the same time, we have the Internet enabling increased control, with its pervasive and collaborative nature. Thus, with a downturned economic cycle, consumers have never been so eager to control their experiences. The virtual world of the Web is now the enabling force to give them this control over their experiences far beyond what they could ever have in the off-line world.

*Source: Growing Through Adversity, Hants RDA Connections; Winter 2009.

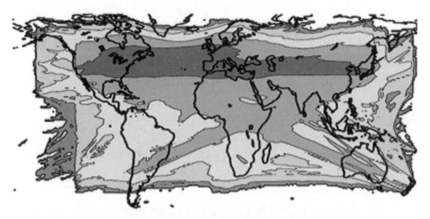

Figure 9.1   A communication heat map

Consider the two main characteristics of the World Wide Web.

Pervasiveness: Currently of the 6,676,120,288 people on the planet, 21.1% of them have Internet access. In this decade alone, this figure has grown by over 300%.*

The Internet's long tentacles surround our globe. This pervasiveness has been statistically documented in a recent study. Microsoft captured anonymized data for one month of the high-level communication activities within Microsoft's entire Messenger instant-messaging system. They tracked 30 billion conversations among 240 million people. From the data they constructed that more than 60,000 email users attempted to reach one of 18 target people in 13 countries by forwarding messages to acquaintances. Their conclusion was that everyone is only six "steps" away from every other person on Earth.**

This is not just a passing phase. The Internet is becoming a foundation tool in people's lives. Information from Vanina Delobelle, PhD, shows:

*http://www.internetworldstats.com/stats.htm.
**Microsoft Research Technical Report – MSR-TR-2006-186 June 2007.

- 41% of Internet users read blogs.
- 47% of the time people spend on the Internet is spent looking at content.
- 33% of the time is spent communicating.

And most telling for businesses:

- 91% of users are likely to buy and make recommendations online.

Ms Delobelle's research also shows the growing importance of social networks:

- Twitter has one million users with three million messages per day.
- Linkedin has 19 million users.
- MySpace has 110 million users.

Collaborative: Originally the Internet was seen as a one-way medium. Consumers could find information; businesses could send out information. That has been transformed. It's now a two-way vehicle that enables collaboration and true conversations.

Given that trust is a core need before a consumer will purchase, the collaborative nature becomes even more important when you consider the Edelman Trust Index on various groups, according to which the following percentages of people expressed trust:

- Public Relations Person – 20%
- CEO – 29%
- Academic – 57%
- Industry analysts – 59%
- Peers – 70%.

The pervasiveness of the Internet makes "word of mouth" exponentially important as it has supercharged consumers' ability to find "someone like me" who is interested in the same product or service.

To give an illustration: A financial institution's customers are critical of the institution during an online discussion. The financial institution does not know how to answer so they reply anonymously. An influential blogger takes note and "buzzes" about it. The buzz increases. The financial institution, now out of control, decides to respond directly but it's too late. The brand damage is done and now it's in crisis management. Without a "get it right and honest the first time" response (rules for successfully being part of the new world), the chance to easily address the issue is gone along with credibility and trust.

Instead of going directly to business for product or service information, consumers are increasingly first going to the Internet. Instead of having a "selling" experience with biased sales and marketing messages, they can control the buying experience. One wherein:

- They need not tolerate the parade of marketing messages whose intent appears to be self-serving.
- They can increase their convenience by buying products and services on their time and their terms.
- They can increase the efficiency of the purchase by researching products first and then having very precise questions for the business.
- They can approach a supplier with greater knowledge and sometimes in greater numbers (which gives them much more room to negotiate).

So given all the challenges and risks to doing business on the net, is it worth it?

There is no question: the economics of this new consumer environment are utterly compelling for almost all industries.

Doing it right

Intuit, the maker of personal finance programs Quicken and TurboTax as well as the small business accounting program QuickBooks, launched a content rich small business network, quickly attracting 90,000 new/unique visitors, i.e. new and existing customers. In the consumer goods industry, Unilever, the makers of Dove soap, launched a viral YouTube video at the cost of a mere $50,000 and created a 30% surge in product sales. In the telecommunications industry, Motorola launched a relatively low-cost viral video campaign in China featuring two young college students which drove new product sales by 270%. A large wireless provider in Europe launched a new product where they cost-effectively identified the "kingpins", i.e. primary influencers in their market, and boosted the new product uptake by 6%.

However while there is potential upside opportunity in this new social marketplace, it is not a forgiving environment.

Doing it wrong

Visa's foray onto Facebook was a great idea but poorly executed. A great plan to initiate new hooks into the small business community was laid waste when promised incentives were unable to be redeemed because of processing issues. As a result, the hopeful new customers became a very disenchanted (and very vocal) group of detractors.

WalMart moved onto Facebook to engage new college students in furnishing their rooms at WalMart via a roommate management facility. It failed. It failed because they were unprepared for their inherent public relations weakness.

Facebook users didn't focus on WalMart's intended value proposition. Instead, the Facebook offering was overrun with criticism.

Ritz-Carlton had a hip new young director create a high profile viral video to extend the image of Ritz-Carlton luxury to a younger generation. They ignored one of the rules of the game: viral videos need to be short and focused. Typically no more than two minutes. They also did not invest sufficient "marketing" of the "marketing", i.e. didn't cross-advertise the YouTube viral video. As a result, only 1700 people viewed the rather expensive video.

Failures have been widespread but predictable. 60% of the failures in trying to enter this new world can be traced to institutions applying the old rules of traditional sales and marketing. 40% of the failures can be attributed to under-investing in the social marketing support.

Succeeding in the social marketplace

For businesses to stay relevant in the new social marketplace, they will need to move from traditional CRM (Customer Relationship Management) to CMR (Customer Managed Relationships). To do this we must first look at the mechanics of the two side-by-side.

Traditional CRM, in its simplest form, follows an established pattern:

- Convert campaigns into leads.
- Use leads to obtain customers/opportunities/contacts.
- Develop customers/opportunities/contacts into meaningful relationships.
- Analyze results to determine success or failure.

CMR is fundamentally a different process:

- Convert content into conversations.
- Shared conversations become collaborative experiences.
- Experiences morph into customers.*

Not only do traditional CRMs and CMRs have distinctly different processes, they have two entirely different approaches. The biggest failure point is when traditional CRM approaches are applied to CMR.

From a structural dimension, these networks are largely leveraged by telecommunication/mobile oriented organizations typically utilizing specific authentication infrastructure as a means to create a physical infrastructure network. For example: AT&T – My Communities, Verizon Wireless – SocialLife.

The mechanics of a CMR fall into the following six dimensions:

- Social Network Segmentation
- Human Needs Linkage
- Approach Mindset
- Dynamics of Satisfaction
- Power in the Text
- Social Network Segmentation.

In using a CMR, the marketplace falls into four categories. Each segment has its own unique characteristics as to who has chosen to be there and why. The four categories are:

Real identities – such as: Linkedin, Facebook, Jigsaw, Spoke Software, and Docstoc where real identities are essential to meeting the members' needs.

Qualitative contacts – at Match.com, PlanetOut Partners, Yahoo match, and Second Chances, members present

---

*Source: Brent Leary.

qualitative characteristics of themselves to find similar or compatible members.

Public exposition – members use YouTube, Flickr, mogulas, qik, MySpace to display aspects of their lives (often for self-promotion) to members and nonmembers.

Fantasized identities – on Second Life, members present adaptations of themselves to adaptations of other members and nonmembers. These annotations range from subtle style variances of their essential selves to wholescale aberrations.

The closer to real identities the network is, the more trust is based on the truth of the identity portrayal. In networks with more fantasized identities, trust is developed based on the fantasized truths. On the surface, this seems counterintuitive. It's not – just as with real identities the key to trust is consistency to the truth; in the fantasy networks it's consistency to the new truths of the fantasized identity.

Truth is critical in all the segments even though the level of truth can be a question within all networks; for example – with real identities: did the member really hold that executive position? With qualitative networks: are the members really the age they say? In the fantasized network consumers can appear with one or many personas or avatars. However, the personas/avatars also reflect a truth about the consumer and given that, plus understanding their human need via digital ID mapping, an organization can maintain relevance and be successful within all social network segments.

Human needs linkage

In the virtual world, consumers can be in one or more or all of the segments. To understand the mechanics of digital

Social Media Landscape

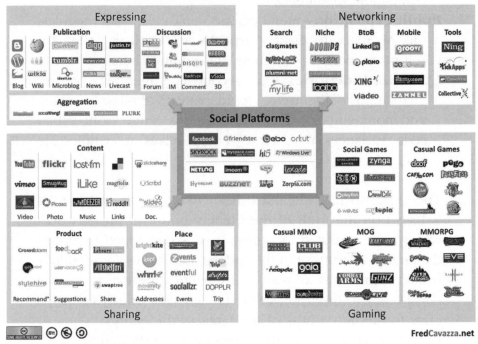

Figure 9.2

IDs it is best to start with "why" people become a member of a particular social network. That will help to identity the member's underlying need. By utilizing Digital ID mapping, it can be determined why a consumer is with any particular social network.

Regardless of the network, a link must be made back to the behavioral needs being met. The best way to do this is to use Maslow's Hierarchy of Needs as a baseline. Applying the Digital ID network type to the different tiers of Maslow's hierarchy will identify the consumer's objective and need. It will also provide insight into how the consumers are likely to buy, and thus enable a business to fulfill the consumers' need.

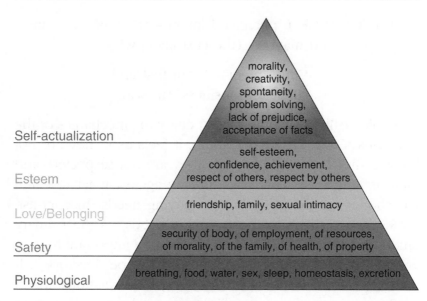

Figure 9.3

Approach mindset

The next critical dimension to being successful within the CMR world is the approach. It cannot be the classic pursuit of the consumer. It not only can't be the "hard" sell, it can't even be a "soft" sell. It needs to be a transparent and subtle "joining a conversation among friends".

In the traditional CRM, the approach was akin to a predator/prey scenario, i.e. we chase you until we catch you. It was force instead of finesse. It could be likened to big game fishing where you sit in the "killing chair" and use huge tackle to force the unwilling fish onto a highly sophisticated boat. CMR is closer to fly-fishing where the fly is "presented" in a very subtle and natural way.

The critical differentiation of these two approaches is the intent.

Traditional CRM: perceived intent – the business wins, and maybe I (the customer) wins.

CMR: intent – I win first and then the business can win.

Psychologically, consumers don't enjoy the mechanics of the traditional CRM "chase". To them, it feels as if they are not known, they are not important, they are not respected, and there is little trust. This goes directly against what research has shown are the basic human buying needs. In contrast, CMR directly aligns to those buying needs, as the primary emotions generated are: you know me, I'm important to you, and you respect me. It also allows trust to be developed. It doesn't have to be an all or nothing trust relationship. In CMR, a consumer can give incremental levels of trust on their terms and according to their timing. The consumer remains in control.

The CMR approach is more of a partnership where a business is a guest in the consumers' world. The value proposition needs to be more compelling and more transparent than traditional CRM approaches. It also must put the consumers' interests first or the intent can be viewed as highly hypocritical, as illustrated in the WalMart example mentioned earlier.

Finally, the CMR approach mindset has a fundamental difference in its objective. Yes, a business needs to make money but the aspiration of keeping a customer for a lifetime is inappropriate and antiquated. It has been most businesses' goal to keep the customers as long as possible while calculating their lifetime value. In CMR, consumers only want to "date", not "get married". During this dating process, they expect to have multiple partners and will only "date" a particular business as long as it provides competitive products and services on their terms – what they want, when, and where they want it.

Dynamics of satisfaction

Within the social marketplace, the concept of loyalty is radically different. Loyalty, as viewed in the physical world, does not exist in the social era. Loyalty exists from one transaction and interaction to the next – that's it. It is similar to the attributes of trust in the social era.

Trust is one of the most critical components of being successful in selling and servicing into this social environment. Very few businesses currently approach trust as a science. To survive the CMR wars, they will need to make a radical change. Successful companies will view trust building not as a name to sit by a product but as an explicit science engineered with process and behavioral sciences intertwined.

Human beings have a cognitive limit as to the number of individuals with whom they can sustain a stable and trusting relationship. This theory emanates from Robin Dunbar, a British anthropologist:

> ... there is a cognitive limit to the number of individuals with whom any one person can maintain stable relationships ... this limit is a direct function of relative neocortex size, and ... this in turn limits group size ... the limit imposed by neocortical processing capacity is simply on the number of individuals with whom a stable inter-personal relationship can be maintained.

The actual cognitive limit for human beings is 100–150 stable relationships. Chimpanzee tribes have a maximum size of 50 chimps. Dunbar theorized that human beings naturally form groups no larger than about 150. This also applies to the networking world.

It manifests itself in a new social hierarchy. Within the social networking world different roles appear. There are "kingpins" who are the major influencers and there are "actors" who are the neutral players. While much of the analysis of social networks move into the qualitative realm of measurement, e.g. demographics to psychographics, it is still important to use quantitative measures for "likelihood to recommend" or net promoter scores to measure the interplay between kingpins and actors. Typically, kingpins would have NPSs (Net Promoter scores) of 9–10 (i.e. be a Net Promoter) or below 5 (i.e. be a Net Detractor). Actors would have neutral NPSs between 6 and 9.

Put into context, Dunbar's theory separates social networks into three categories:

Creative Network

- Groups of approximately 12 members
- Dynamic closes to sharing a "dinner conversation"
- Participation tends to be dense and equal.

Social Network

- Groups of approximately 150 members
- Dynamic is closest to classic group dynamics
- Participation tends to follow a traditional bell curve.

Political Network

- Groups can number in the thousands of members
- Communication is closest to mass media
- Participation tends to be random, scale-free, and reflect less consistency by members.*

Within Dunbar's theory, there are variations on levels of satisfaction as actors expand or contract the number of rela-

*Source: Ross Mayfield.

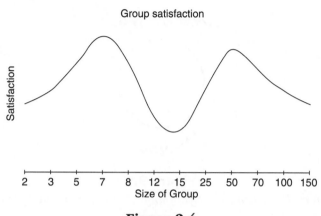

Figure 9.4

Source: Robin Dunbar theory.

tionships. This requires a significant change in how customer satisfaction is viewed, as the traditional view of customer satisfaction is a linear picture with no consideration of group size.

Also traditionally customer satisfaction is a reflective interest. Within the social market it needs to be upfront in the thinking. The current level and the optimum satisfaction within a particular group will need to be considerations in how (and if) a business will enter a specific social networkers' world.

Another way of describing the dynamics of this social phenomenon is with a circle of trust. Businesses need to think of their actions relative to entering the social network's circle of trust. Initially, they will be on the outside looking in.

There is however one aspect of the traditional marketplace that continues within the social marketplace. That is the different levels of trust afforded humans versus machines. It's the difference currently seen between the trust given a call center rep or a bank teller and that given to IVRs, ATMs, and Internet banking. Human beings are seven times as intolerant of machines as they are of human beings. In other

Figure 9.5
Source: Evolutionary Psychology – Dundar, Barrett, Lycett.

words, people will grant other people conditional trust, allowing for mistakes. To err is human. There is no such allowance for "machines". This makes the "cost of quality" high when Internet execution is done poorly, i.e. not done right the first time and every time. As well, the more closely the electronic device is linked to the identity of the human, e.g. mobile telephone, the less tolerant that human is. This is why it is critically important when a business enters the networking realm in the mobile phone environment; they do so carefully as mobile phones have a high level of correlation to an individual's self-identity.

Power in the text

"Give me 26 lead soldiers and I will conquer the world." Ben Franklin knew a printing press with 26 letters had more power than guns in the American Revolution. Karl Marx had the same insight. The written words of both men brought about profound changes. Companies can also use the written word to bring change to their business if they harness the power of text on the Internet. Today, and more so in the future, knowledge will predominantly come in the form of text conversations, not face-to-face dialogues.

It is obvious that within the social marketplace, text is all-important. Equally obvious are the challenges to effectively utilizing it. It can be stated in the alphabet string: "IDKWILFBIKIWISI" or in full: "I Don't Know What I'm Looking For, But I'll Know It When I See It". That's a small example of how powerful text analytic tools are needed to not only understand the text but also the relationships between words, phrases, and fragments.

A couple of useful tools in unlocking the secrets of the consumer conversations are:

- Segment analysis with Neuro-Linguistic Programming
- Link analysis of Influence Ranking.

Segment analysis using Neuro-Linguistic Programming (NLP)

Neuro-Linguistic Programming describes the fundamental dynamics between mind (neuro) and language (linguistic) and how their interplay affects our body and behavior (programming). It covers the three most influential components for understanding and producing the human experience:

- Neurology – regulates how our bodies function
- Language – determines how we interface and communicate with other people
- Programming – describes the fundamental dynamics between mind and behavior.

NLP can be applied effectively in the analysis of text to identify the relationships between words and sentiment and their influence in specific communities.*

*References: Richard Bandler, John Grinder, Gregory Bateson.

Link analysis of influence ranking

Understanding the dynamics of influence, including the degree of authority of the influencer, is an important tool to utilizing text. Influence can be defined as the intentional or unintentional affect an influencer has on the actions or beliefs of the subject. Authority is the amount of "weight" one person's view has versus another person's. Link analysis can be applied to locate influential individuals by their level of engagement with a supplier of products or services. It can also be used as an alert mechanism to tell a business at what level of authority or influence they need to act. Thirdly, it can be used as a weighting metric for features by a specific author, e.g. a blogger within the system.

Beyond these two analytical tools, there are other subtleties which are important to understand within the utilization of text. With influencers, both positive and negative, there are the issues of:

- Target – what does the text reference.
- Rhetorical purpose – what is the role of the text, e.g. to introduce a topic, support an argument, expand a discussion.
- Subjectivity – what is the text's position: positive or negative.

All are important in identifying and understanding influencers and their text. These are difficult challenges but challenges that can be overcome. The solution is not to just address the text, but to address the context of the text. That is where subjectivity is the key.

To operate within the social network world a business needs to understand that subjectivity (particularly of high influencers) can have as much or more impact than fact. Therefore, it is necessary to understand the schematic of subjectivity and be able to utilize text to assess it. There are three fundamental levels of subjectivity:

- Statement – e.g. Strawberries taste better than raspberries.
- Opinion – e.g. Henry should eat strawberries instead of raspberries.
- Sentiment – e.g. I love strawberries.

All three levels of subjectivity reflect the influencer's opinion to various degrees of intensity.

Online opinions have three qualities:

- Invariant – the property of a text which is similar in all texts of a given author and different in texts from other authors.
- Latent – the contextual usage and meaning of words.
- Synthetic – the synthesized opinion from the words and context.

Opinions can be expressed either directly as stand-alone comments or can be implicit in other statements. The current constraint in analyzing opinions is that text can be attributed to an opinion but not to a particular person.

The opinion process

Impetus – Synthesis – Expression – Interpretation – Re-expression

It starts with the impetus (what drove them). Then there is the synthesis (assimilations of their thoughts), followed by the expression (communicating it), followed by the inter-pretation (someone reads it and applies their own under-standing) and finally it's re-expressed and the process begins again with the re-expressing reader. In this way, opinions can be transferred and can seem to be "contagious".

When looking at opinions regarding a particular business, there are a number of factors at play:

- the individual's beliefs;
- their personality;
- the influences they are under or exert;
- their particular authority in recommending (or not) the business;
- and the context of the specific community that shares that belief.

All these factors weigh heavily. These concepts are then communicated in words, phrases, fragments, URLs, and threads, which get transformed by the perception and interpretation of others.*

In conclusion, utilizing text to analyze the subjectivity of the content and the influence within the social media data is a necessity for financial institutions who wish to be relevant and thus successful within the social marketplace.

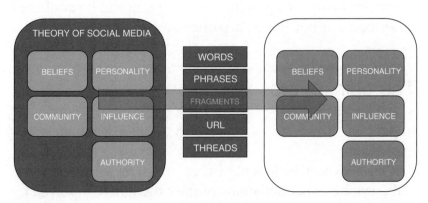

Figure 9.6

*Reference: Matt Hewhurst, Live Labs, Microsoft.

Building a business case for the Web

Just as traditional CRMs don't apply to the social marketplace, so too business cases and performance metrics need to be altered. The bottom line though is the same: bottom-line sales, expenses, and ROI are what ultimately count.

In addition, if sales are not to be completed on the website, then leads needs to be a primary metric. A campaign that only brings page views but no new potential clients isn't going to deliver the results needed.

Beyond those traditional measures, many others should be utilized in a web business case and/or ongoing assessment of performance:

1. **Conversions** – While conversions may take the form of people joining a network, participating in a forum, recommending a website or simply subscribing to a blog. These are all conversions that make a very reliable website or marketing campaign success metric.

2. **Subscribers** – While subscribers can be considered conversions, they also can be counted themselves right as every site should offer RSS and thus, track RSS as well as email subscriptions just like blogs do. Subscribers are a business's most important website, even if they do not buy anything.

3. **Usability metrics** – While not every site's success can be measured in revenue, sales, or leads, a business always can and should measure the sheer usability of their site. Many sites today still concentrate on being visually pleasing, "having a bigger logo", and some special effects like Flash or AJAX, sound, or video. While this might look good in most cases it's not the most important factor that decides whether your site is going to fail or to succeed – usability is.

4. **Returning visitors** – When visitors return, they communicate that they like the site. So the more visitors who come back the better, i.e. the more successful you are. One-time search visitors and casual social media visitors are not the backbone of a site. The subscribers and returning visitors (often the same people) are.

5. **Page views per visit** – While measuring page views is sometimes meaningless as poorly designed websites can cause the visitor to click many places to get to the relevant pages, the number of page views per visit often will tell a business what visitors like about the site. A 1 to 1 ratio is bad unless they all click the buy button instantly.

6. **Time on page** – The time spent on a page can be measured in many ways. Primarily it provides an indication of whether people just skim the content or read it in depth.

7. **Time on site** – It is not always the case that the longer someone spends on your site, the better it is for your website. Five minutes is in most cases better than 30 seconds, though, especially for a publishing site or simply a blog.

8. **Bounce rate** – Bounce rate is one of the most important usability metrics and, thanks to Google Analytics or Woopra, an easy metric to follow. 100k visitors from Digg with a bounce rate of 95% means that in fact only 5000 visited the site. So a site with a much lower visitor number *and* bounce rate can be much more successful than a less intelligent "traffic" site with large traffic numbers. Targeted quality traffic is critical for a successful site.

9. **Form/shopping cart abandonment rate** – Forms are the most important features of websites in business terms, e.g. contact form, shopping cart (technically a form). Now imagine a supermarket where more than

half of the customers abandon their cart in the middle of the checkout process or while perusing the market.

10. **Next pages** – Internal links are used to encourage people to visit more than one page on a site. Some of the links are designed for people to follow to other pages. By checking the "next pages" from a particular landing page, it can be determined whether the readers followed the design or wanted to see more of it.

11. **Links clicked (heat maps)** – Modern "Web 2.0" web analytics solutions offer heat maps views or, at minimum, a site overlay way of checking clicks. This provides information on where visitors click or try to click

12. **Eye-tracking** – Tracking "eyes" is more effective than heat maps of click behavior as eye-tracking is the tracking of actual eye movements. This requires visitors to take part in a study. However, it can provide invaluable insight into where they instinctively look and what they see on a given website.

13. **Internal searches** – Visitors can be random or targeted. This information is available by analyzing internal searches. Google Analytics allows this and there are even widgets developed to do this.

14. **SEO (Search Engine Optimization) metrics** – SEO experts are totally focused on measuring searches. They measure PageRank, rankings, and traffic. And there are quite a few search measurements beyond strict business or usability metrics. Old school SEO still makes sense in many cases, especially with backlinks. Backlinks still determine a site's success within Google search. In the US market, it also makes sense to check these with Yahoo and others.

15. **Number of backlinks** – In addition it's beneficial to know how many people or pages link to a business site especially if that number is changing.

16. **Quality of backlinks** – Counting backlinks can be meaningless unless they are quality backlinks. This can be determined by measuring how many outgoing links the linking page has. Whether it has PageRank or is an old authority domain are also indicators.

17. **Google cache date** – Many SEO specialists fall back to checking the cache date in Google (Google saves most pages in a "cache") for determining the quality and success of a website in Google. If the cache date is older than one month the site is either dead (old content) or has a very low authority/relevancy with Google.

18. **Google bot (robot) visit frequency** – A cache may be one week old, but if a Google bot visits the cache daily, it's relevant. Most server side web analytics tools (those relying on server logs or PHP) can provide this data.

19. **Last time Google bot visited** – This is similar to the above example, the difference being that if there is a new content page and the bot visited yesterday and the site doesn't show in the Google index something might be wrong (like duplicate content problems).

20. **Pages indexed** – Determining the value of pages indexed is more complicated than just assuming that "the more pages indexed the better", unless you are a smaller site. If there are 50 pages online but only 20 indexed, the site is not successfully spidered by Google. A site:yoursite.com search in Google will assist with this measure.

21. **PageRank "pass rate"** – Google PageRank is passed via the links on a website. A home page with PR 5 should have subpages with PR 4 or at least 3, otherwise there are too many links and/or the internal link structure is broken.

22. **Alexa Rank** – While Alexa's reliability may be questionable, many advertisers use it to check a site's traffic numbers. Alexa traffic estimates can also be compared to other sites, other time periods (e.g. year over year), and other traffic estimation tools.

23. **Compete Rank** – Compete may be more reliable than Alexa but it is limited to US web traffic.

24. **Social Media metrics** – In the age of social media, tracking user generated content may be difficult for a business as they cannot rely solely on bots and other automatically gathered numbers to collect data on their website's success.

25. **Bookmarks on Delicious** – A site or page with a few hundred or thousand bookmarks on Delicious is generally deemed as a good sign of a site's health but insufficient to determine a site's effectiveness without other metric context.

26. **Bookmarks elsewhere** – While it is fairly simple to hire a service to submit your website to bookmark sites like Delicious etc. it's far more likely that a site is a good one if it is popular on Delicious as well as other bookmark sites.

27. **Social news submissions** – Submissions are a better measurement of your site's popularity and its straight visits.

28. **Tweets (Twitter mentions)** – Being mentioned or recommended on Twitter is a true success because people communicate with their peers ("people like them") and followers. As a result, they only link pages that they would truly recommend to a friend. Being linked more than two or three times means you are an influencer and respected. It means two or three people telling 100 or maybe 200 other people. TweetBeep will send you an email each time.

29. **Niche social news site votes** – In marketing circles and for SEO blogs it is widely known that the search marketing social news site Sphinn is the destination to submit your work. Being successful here means recognition by experts and highly targeted visitors. Each niche has its own niche social news site: Hugg for "green" news, YCombinator for startups and technology, Design Float and Design Bump for design, and DZone for web development and programming.

30. **Number of "thumbs up" on StumbleUpon** – Other than Digg or Reddit, social browsing sites like StumbleUpon are populated by the general public from around the globe. People voting for a site on StumbleUpon "like you". Whether a site has "mass appeal" can be discovered here (not on Digg).

31. **StumbleUpon reviews feedback** – People who write reviews about a site on StumbleUpon have a real emotional connection to the site, the StumbleUpon community, and/or the subject they are addressing. Getting 10 or more "awesome" reviews on StumbleUpon is a solid measurement regarding the overall popularity of a website or a particular webpage.

32. **Technorati Blog mentions** – A page often mentioned on Technorati is truly admired in the blogosphere. The Technorati authority is not a reliable metric. It's based largely on Technorati bookmarks, which bloggers can manipulate easily.

33. **Google BlogSearch Links** – While the main Google search does not show many links, the Google blogsearch does. It will show the legitimate links by other blogs, not the scraper blogs. The scraper blogs (bloggers who gather copyrighted material) can be monitored by using AideRSS.*

*Source: 33 Website Success Metrics (Tad Chef).

Summary

This new social consumer era represents the ultimate in dichotomies – everything must change in how businesses sell, market, and service consumers yet nothing has changed in the basic consumer fundamentals. Consumers have crossed the power precipice fueled by the Internet and the information it embodies yet their underlying buying fundamentals have not changed.

As rational consumers, they still want the best product at the best price but now it's in an era fueling commoditization. As intuitive human beings, the social era has heightened their sense of importance, deepened their sense of self-respect, and placed a new priority on mutual trust for how and from whom they buy.

In the current economic environment this provides an excellent opportunity for a business if (and it's a big if) they are able to enter the social marketplace quickly, honestly, and within the guidelines mentioned.

"Homerun" social network case study – Dove Evolution

Unilever launched a viral marketing campaign in 2006 as part of its Dove Campaign for Real Beauty, to promote the newly created Dove Self-Esteem Fund. The focal point of the Unilever campaign was a 75-second spot produced by Ogilvy & Mather in Toronto, Canada. The viral marketing video was first displayed online on 6 October 2006, and was later broadcast as a television and cinema spot in the Netherlands and the Middle East. The ad was created from the budget left over from the earlier Daughters campaign, and was intended to be the first in a series of such online-focused spots by the company. It has been discussed in many mainstream television programs and print publications, and the exposure generated by the spot has been estimated to be worth over $150 million.

The film opens with a "pretty, but ordinary girl" entering and sitting down in a studio. The camera switches to a time lapse sequence, showing a team of people adding make-up and adjusting the hair of the woman, transforming her into a "beautiful billboard model". Then a series of "Photoshopping" adjustments are made to alter the appearance of the model further. The final image is displayed on a billboard. The short movie finishes by displaying text saying "No wonder our perception of beauty is distorted."

From the beginning, Dove transcended the classic "products sell" and focused on its "higher calling" looking beyond the Hollywood definition of beauty and supporting the inner beauty in every young woman. The message was simple, the content was pure, the conversation was of the highest level, and it was all about the consumer … about their life, their esteem. And most of all, it was on their terms. The natural virality and consumer advocacy spawned by the movie short was nothing short of inspiring, as was the movie itself.

Figure 9.7

Quality of Content (value-add)   10
Quality of Conversation   10
On Consumer's terms   10
Virality/Advocacy   10

The bottom line was Buying Behavior Increased by 40%.

Other stats:
Added: October 6, 2006
Views: 9,560,548
Ratings: 9,966
Comments: 4,526
Favorited: 35,569 times
Length: 1:15.

The actual dollar figure to create this viral marketing was $120,000 US. They calculated that it costs them $.00657 per view which was a better ROI than from a marketing campaign run during the Super Bowl. Not only did product sales skyrocket but also their brand stature increased.

This was a home run. Can financial institutions hope to achieve such a lofty win? Likely not. Can financial institutions use the same fundamentals to achieve great success in CMR? Unequivocally yes.

For financial institutions, entry into CMR is not a question – it's the way the world is going and nothing will stop its evolution. It is a strategic imperative that institutions get into this while doing the due diligence required to make the first inroads positive and thus, serve as a launch point to further initiatives.

Wells Fargo's bold "social" move

The financial institution that has made the boldest entry into social networking is Wells Fargo. They've instituted a

Figure 9.8

multiple network, e.g. Facebook, MySpace, YouTube, corporate blogs, approach including:

The Student LoanDown – Financing/debt
Guided By History – Historical archives
Stagecoach Island Community – Game
Commercial Electronic Office – Ideas.

Their innovative foray into CMR covers a broad range – all the way from reality to fantasy. The reality initiative is closer to basic real world financing and debt management for students. The Stagecoach Island community is more of a gaming approach, which subtly intertwines financial management learning to a gaming environment. The premise is that the fantasy figure "Cassie" will promote the social networking aspects of their site while subtly intertwining financial education and general fun. "Stagecoach Island" is a virtual world where members role-play games such as general socializing or building a dream house. Guests do this by exploring the "Stagecoach Island" and its hidden secrets, connecting with friends and making new ones and all the while, they're painlessly learning about money management.

Wells Fargo also instituted a contest entitled "Win Someday" which is popular with YouTube followers. The basic premise is that "Everybody's got a dream for Someday" and that you can display your dream with your own video to win the "Someday contest".

1. Quality of Content (value-add) 5
2. Quality of Conversation 4
3. On Consumer's terms 8
4. Virality/Advocacy 7

Royal Bank goes back to school

Royal Bank demonstrated an innovative approach by launching a financial advice blog written by students ... for students. Fans can access the page via Facebook – "RBC Bankbook". Royal Bank selected six full-time post-secondary students from Canadian universities to write daily blogs on money management. There are also videos available on the bank's website. How better to engage your target market than to employ the market itself?

1. Quality of Content (value-add) 7
2. Quality of Conversation 8
3. On Consumer's terms 9
4. Virality/Advocacy 7

Scotiabank's staff goes social

Scotiabank decided to leverage the power of the social dynamic internally for their staff. The Web 2.0 attributes enabled (with the appropriate privacy and security mechanisms) information sharing and collaboration amongst the staff. Employees were able to share, store, organize, search, and manage information using blogs and wikis. The sharing of best practices and the identification of experts and skill sets regardless of geographic and organizational boundaries were part of the successful results. Wikis, blogs, and RSS feeds were all part of the enabling technology. To extend the capabilities of this knowledge sharing, they employed a customizable and security-enhanced interface.

1. Quality of Content (value-add)   7
2. Quality of Conversation   7
3. On Employee's terms   8
4. Virality/Advocacy   7

Comparisons

It is quite helpful to look at different social marketing initiatives relative to the distinct approaches and their resulting outcomes. This is a comparison of three: Amex's Open Forum, Advanta's Ideablog, and QuickBooks Community.

Amex's Open Forum

This essentially is a business forum and resource directory. To heighten the appeal, American Express added posts from several prominent bloggers on topical small business subjects, e.g. John Battelle's Searchblog, Anita Campbell's Small Biz Trends. They have had a reasonable uptake – 15,400 members, and a monthly traffic of about 55,000 unique visitors – up five times from a year ago.

1. Quality of Content (value-add)   7
2. Quality of Conversation   6
3. On Consumer's terms   6
4. Virality/Advocacy   6

Advanta's Ideablob

Advanta, which focuses on small business credit cards, instituted a unique small business idea contest where people could submit small business ideas and win $10,000. The concept was to create a living breathing community of ideas under the banner – Ideablob. Their offer was "Submit your idea. Get votes. Win $10,000." While contests are relatively common in the social networking world, it was a unique approach to offer this in the small business arena, to have monthly contests awarding $10,000 to the best idea. These ideas were voted on by the users. The website had reasonable traction with about 30,000 unique visitors according to Compete.

1. Quality of Content (value-add)   3
2. Quality of Conversation   3
3. On Consumer's terms   4
4. Virality/Advocacy   6

QuickBooks Community

QuickBooks (Intuit) launched an online community leveraging its already active physical community. The online community has strong content and active blogs in the different expertise and industry areas. It is rich with content and touts 10 specialized blogs. They currently have significant traffic with 90,000 unique visitors. That number has doubled from the previous year.

1. Quality of Content (value-add)   7
2. Quality of Conversation   8
3. On Consumer's terms   8
4. Virality/Advocacy   7

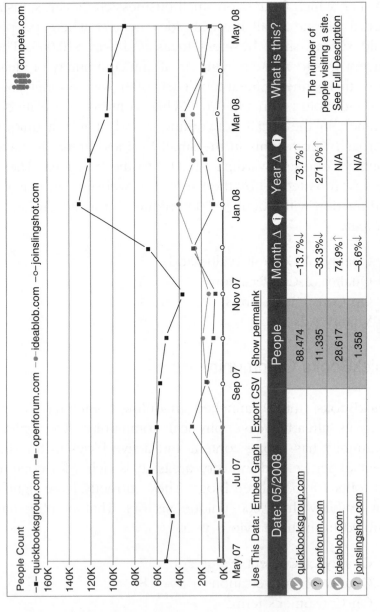

Figure 9.9

When you compare and contrast the approaches and the outcome in terms of activity, it is clear why Quick-Books' success far exceeds Advanta's and AMEX's. To begin with, they started off with a more robust physical community so the launch point was easier. Secondly, they focused on specialized and rich content for each one of the specialty areas with enough purpose-built blogs to enable people to feel like they are with "someone like me".

TD Canada Trust not writing for the two-way street

TD Canada Trust initiated "SPLIT IT" on Facebook, which allowed roommates on Facebook to manage how they split bills (Figure 9.10). Their Facebook page links to their Money Lounge which has job postings, videos, and other offers.

Figure 9.10

They started off with a reasonable uptake of 1480 members. But they were not prepared for the criticism that came from the members about how the application lacked functionality and features – "we didn't anticipate that". The employees who were monitoring and facilitating the conversation were not prepared to participate: "... chats are going on instantaneously; you have people criticizing the bank, and in some cases asking questions". Employees were asking, "Please tell us what we can tell them, help us." The bank reacted quickly (within 48 hours) and appropriately by creating a group to monitor the criticisms and questions and coach on the feedback.

It's a major challenge to truly add value to the demographics of Facebook users. The critical question though is how to maintain the truth of your brand and yet not be seen as pandering to the Facebook demographic.

1. Quality of Content (value-add)   4
2. Quality of Conversation   3
3. On Consumer's terms   4
4. Virality/Advocacy   5

Visa's first face on Facebook

Visa created a new Visa business network on Facebook. As part of the launch, they advertised it by giving away $2 million in Facebook advertising credits. Visa would give $100 advertising credit to each of the first 20,000 new members. They had an initial reasonable uptake of 70,184 monthly active users (up from 23,000). Users rated the new business network 2.9 of 5 up from 2.6 based on 83 reviews.

Visa's value proposition was to "[c]onnect with other small business owners, learn ways to manage your business more efficiently, and grow by reaching the millions of potential customers on Facebook". One of Visa's downfalls was that the Facebook page looked very "corporate" – not in line with the Facebook demographic.

And there was one other slight problem – new members couldn't navigate the process sufficiently to obtain the $100 advertising credit. This caused a flurry of bad press:

- "No Coupon."
- "I signed up but same here ... no coupon for me too."
- "Still no coupon no coupon no coupon no coupon."
- "This is ridiculous ... how many folks have the same complaint!!!"
- "I got mine immediately."
- "No mention of ANY kinds of discounts or free offers once I took the trouble to sign up and give Visa all my personal info."
- "Seems like nice service, but isn't that just classic crummy sales approach to sucker you in with something free and then once you sign up, there's no mention of, or any links to, the offer. They just leave you hanging. I guess we just put our faith in the big corporation and hope it gets around to sending these coupons."

This negative reaction was heightened by how much it asked of its new members to participate informationally. To actually receive their $100 credit, new members had to allow the Visa application to ...

- Know who they were and have access to their information
- Put a box in their profile
- Place a link in their left-hand navigation
- Publish stories in their News Feed and Mini-Feed
- Place a link below the profile picture on any profile
- Send them notifications via email.

The whole experience tried to break the first rule of the social marketplace – the customer has control.

Another mistake, a common mistake, was the response to the negative comments. It was too slow in coming. Ultimately, they realized that to come out with an honest apology and a solution to the problem was the best way to mitigate the damage and turn things around to a positive.

Visa's response was: "Having trouble receiving your ad credit? We apologize if you're having trouble getting your $100 ad credit. We could have done a better job of communicating the necessary steps. To receive the ad credits, you must do three things:

(1)   Add the application
(2)   Fill out a Visa Business Network profile. Completing the business profile triggers the email containing the $100 ad coupon code.
(3)   Check the inbox of the email you used to sign up for Facebook for your coupon code."

1.   Quality of Content (value-add)   3
2.   Quality of Conversation   3
3.   On Consumer's terms   2
4.   Virality/Advocacy   5

Bank of America attempts to be social

Bank of America started its Small Business Online Community as one of its initial attempts at social networking. Launched in late 2007, it was the format of a general forum and resource directory. Basically, it was a forum with some additional articles on the side. Total membership was around 15,000. It was a reasonable attempt at entering the social networking arena. Relative to other advertising investments, however it was minuscule.

Bank of America also tried an initiative with Facebook entitled "MedalMe". The format was that you would recognize a friend or colleague for a specific accomplishment and Bank of America would award them a gold, silver, or bronze medal.

"Do you have a friend who deserves special recognition for an accomplishment, an action, or just being a great buddy? Award the friend a gold, silver, or bronze medal, and describe what the award is for. What a great way to say: 'Well done!'

The problem was that there was virtually no linkage to the bank's products and services – to its business.

1. Quality of Content (value-add)   3
2. Quality of Conversation   3
3. On Consumer's terms   2
4. Virality/Advocacy   4

10 Summary

Business's greatest customer opportunities and risks are determined by how well customers are managed through economic cycles. In the broadest context, predicting and preparing for economic cycles and transitions are a critical component to organizations. They can start by learning from the powerful lessons of the past as many of the same behaviors are repeated over time. The key to predicting economic cycles is to regularly monitor the market's collective consciousness through regional surveys. The key to planning for these realities is creating planning scenarios that span the entire range of economic possibilities. An important part of this planning is to learn from the collective hindsights of organizations where proactive strategies to economic cycles invariably outperform reactive actions. Once the broader economic cycles are planned for, the science of how consumer buying changes must be understood and applied, the first dimension being how they reprioritize their low (rational) and high-order (intuitive/human) needs over changing economic cycles. The second dimension is how consumers create the perception of value over economic cycles and transitions. The third overarching dimension is how economic conditions dramatically affect the first two dimensions. One of the most dramatic pressures of economic cycles is its impact on customer loyalty. This makes it critical for organizations to first understand what types of loyalty they are creating and how those types of loyalty will weather different economic transitions. Effective business strategies for any economic cycle or transition should be designed for a particular economic condition or transition – whether that be boom, bust, or transitioning in or out of either of those two conditions. The skills and competencies needed for B2C center up more around the behavioral psychology of how buying dynamics change over economic conditions. The B2B strategies should not only focus on building compelling business cases for the changing dynamics of how business customers change their spending emphasis but also on business transformation opportunities beyond a myopic view of their market. All of these critical strategies and approaches rely on an organization's ability to leverage its information to maximize opportunities and minimize risks through economic transitions. An overarching critical component to an organization's effectiveness is how well they manage their employees through economic cycles. The critical awareness is that they are real people under parallel stresses and dynamics of economic conditions and should be managed accordingly. As with any change which brings added stress, the power of the community should be leveraged to its maximum potential – both the physical community around the organization and the ever evolving online community.

Index

*Index compiled by Annette
  Musker*